Actually, I'm English

rediscovering my homeland on foot and by motorbike

by

Nick Adams

Copyright © 2015 Nick Adams

All rights reserved.

ISBN-13: 978-1523332854

ISBN-10: 1523332859

CONTENTS

PREFACE

PART 1: Cardiff to Conway – the Cambrian Way

PART 2: Edale to Kirk Yetholm – the Pennine Way

PART 3: Around England by Royal Enfield

PART 4: Bits and Pieces – Wales, Peak District, Lakes

PART 5: Coast to Coast – Cloughton to St. Bees

PART 6: Back on the Bike – Another Royal Enfield

POSTSCRIPT

Nick Adams

PREFACE

Years ago, I was told a story about a man from Cornwall who had left his home county and moved to Norfolk to work. After a pint or two he became a bit melancholy and was heard to say (and you have to imagine this in the broadest of West Country accents),

'I been 'ere fordy year, and oy'm still a bloody foreigner'.

I know exactly what he meant. In another couple of years, I will have been living in Canada for *'fordy year'* and while I rarely feel like a foreigner now, *'no matter how fair these foreign hills may be, they are not the hills of home'* (Andy Stewart – A Scottish Solider).

I miss my home land. I miss the times I spent hiking in northern England, Wales, and Scotland. I miss the pubs. I miss hearing people speaking in incomprehensible regional dialects, all of whom are convinced they're speaking the Queen's English. I miss being surrounded by historic buildings, ancient monuments and walking on soil which has been enriched by countless generations of my ancestors.

The following chapters are short accounts of some of my trips back to the UK; a UK which has changed over the years, as have I. I can't promise any great insights into those changes as they have been evolutionary in nature.

As the years have passed, I have gradually become more North American in my dress, my attitudes and even in the way I sound.

For good or ill, I have become somewhat separated from the land of my birth. These walks and rides are my rediscoveries.

PART 1

THE CAMBRIAN WAY
- CARDIFF TO CONWAY-

Getting Started

I spent the first half an hour of the journey from Gatwick to Cardiff trying to put my finger on the odour permeating the train. At first, its acrid edge made me think it was some industrial smell, dragged in through the carriage windows. Then I wondered whether it could be a arm pit residue left by sweaty soccer fans, making their drunken exhausted way home from Arsenal or Fulham. Finally, after much deliberating, I came to the conclusion that it was the smell of stale urine.

The smell didn't seem to emanate from any one place; indeed, while the toilet at the end of the carriage had its own pungent mix of typical bathroom delights, the carriage smell was no more prevalent within the toilet than without. Numerous feet must have transported spilled pee along the corridors, and over time, the smell had worked its way into all the fittings and furniture. Once I had the smell pegged, I was able to relax and enjoy the rest of the journey.

I had flown out of Toronto the previous evening, taking off shortly before midnight on the twenty first of March. This trip wasn't the product of extensive planning. Three weeks before, I had been moping around, avoiding work and generally making everyone around me miserable when Christine suggested that I took a hike.

I had been grumpy and unresponsive for days. Chris and I had barely been speaking to one another and when we had it was strained. For a few years my moods had been swinging like a pendulum, particularly towards the end of the winter when the Ontario snow lingers too long and the world looks bleak and used up. Hiking is a means of escape. I knew that once I got started I wouldn't be thinking about clients, projects, deadline's or any of the other concerns that plague me from day to day. My concerns would be refined to those of food, feet, footing and where I will lay my head.

Canada to Cardiff

The plane journey had been tedious and uneventful, involving too much time languishing in airports and too much time in the cramped confines of the aeroplane, eating dubious in-flight meals with my knees jammed into the seat back ahead of me. I think the gnomes who layout the interior of long distance jet liners must take their archetypal human form from Thailand or Japan. My six foot two inch frame simply doesn't fit the allotted space.

Astonishingly, the transition from the plane, through baggage retrieval and customs went remarkably quickly. My rucksack had been placed with other oversized and awkward objects for special handling, and I was expecting to have to struggle to get it back, but it arrived at the same time as all the other suitcases, allowing me to make a speedy exit for the train station. Within a few moments, I had bought my ticket and was on the train to Cardiff.

It was already after three in the afternoon before I arrived in Cardiff. The station disgorges you virtually in to the heart of the city, but once I figured out which way was north, I was able to head up St. Mary's Street towards Cardiff Castle and the start of the Cambrian Way in Bute Park. My main objective was to put miles behind me and leave the city behind. I don't like the darn things at the best of times and I had no intention of spending my first night in the suburbs.

My walk through Bute Park started off inauspiciously. As I changed into my hiking footwear and prepared for some serious walking, I was hit by a barrage of steamy rhetoric from a passing gentleman. I'll give him the benefit of the doubt and assume that he was simply drunk, although I think it far more likely that he was suffering from some more permanent malady.

The trail through Bute Park sticks fairly close to the River Taff and is well used by dog-walkers, cyclists, roller-bladers, hikers and stroller pushing mums. Two of the first cyclists to pass me were having an animated conversation in Welsh. This was a big surprise. During my teenage years I had spent many weeks cycling and hiking throughout Wales, and the Welsh language had never been anything more than a very quiet background hum. You might have heard two old ladies chatting in Welsh at a rural post office, but they would nearly always switch to English as soon as they saw you, as if caught in some subversive act. Now, I could hear the Welsh language was everywhere. There have certainly been some changes over the last forty years.

I'm sure Cardiff Castle is nice enough but I wasn't in Wales to explore relics, at least, not so soon off the train, so I continued to follow the trail along the river past kids playing cricket and soccer. Finding a secluded place for a pee was a bit of a problem. No sooner would I throw my pack down and start to fumble with my zipper than someone would be along. I wondered if Britain had become so crowded whether I would be able to find the peace and solitude I used to enjoy.

Misreading the map, I took an unscheduled diversion into the suburbs which surround the park. By this point, having been awake since early the previous morning, I was getting tired, irritable and my pack was beginning to feel heavy, so straying off what was really a very straight forward route, while daft, wasn't too surprising. After stumbling around some side streets for a while, I managed to get back on course, found the Glamorgan Canal tow-path, and headed towards the M4 interchange just south of Tongwynlais.

The guidebook of the Cambrian Way suggests that navigating through the interchange can be testing - I found it surprisingly straightforward. The road I took passed the village of Tongwynlais and through heavily wooded hills, looking dark and mysterious in the gloomy evening. By this point I was almost dead on my feet, so after instructing a clueless youth on how best to handle his errant Doberman pup ("no - don't hit it when it finally comes back to you, you are just teaching it to stay away...."), I headed into Fforest Fawr to find a place to sleep.

I practice what I like to think of as 'stealth camping'; the objective being to arrive late, use the minimum of equipment, be gone before anyone notices, and leave no trace. No fires, no noise -except perhaps for a bit of snoring. Up to that point the weather had been clear and warm, and being naturally lazy, I deliberated whether to put up my shelter or just roll out my sleeping bag in the ferns and brambles. In the end, caution prevailed, I hastily threw up my bivvy, brought all my gear inside and fell quickly to sleep.

Up to Abergavenny

I awoke to the mild but steady pattering or rain. From my sleeping bag I could hear the Mistle Thrushes singing, telling me that it would soon be over, and by the time I had broken camp, the rain was gone and the sun was starting to emerge. This would be the first real day of my hike. The previous day had been too much of a blur of planes, trains and suburbs for me to really consider it part of the journey - just the necessary evils of travel to get you from where you were to where you want to be.

My route led through pastures and woodlands, through Machen and Crosskeys, following the Rhymney Valley Ridgeway for much of the distance. Although clearly well travelled, I had the path entirely to myself as I passed through the mature beech woods which follow the ridge, before descending on forest roads to Machen.

By the time I reached Machen, my internal clock was warning me that lunchtime had passed some time ago, so I was delighted to find a pub. I deposited my pack in the vestibule, changed my muddy boots for my running shoes, walked in to the bar and taken aback by the landlords reaction.

"Can I help you?" he said, in that tone that really means, "What the heck are you doing here?".

"I'd like a pint of bitter please?"

"We don't open 'till 12" he said, still looking at me as though I was a few bricks short of a load.

After years in Canada, my previously impeccable BBC English has become diluted with enough of a North American twang that whenever I open my mouth, people in Britain now assume that I am American. This is definitely not a good thing. Despite an almost pathological devotion to Dallas re-runs, Oprah and Dr. Phil - or perhaps because of it - your average Brit treats those from the other side of the Atlantic as they would, harmless, but slightly retarded cousins. During my exile, I have returned to Britain many times, and as my accent has changed, so has the way people have spoken to me.

I should emphasize that I have never been treated with anything but kindness. But whether looking for directions to the railway station, or trying to decide on which beer to buy, the helpful suggestions have almost always been provided as if addressing a rather dull five year old. Nobody has actually sounded out the letters yet, but it wouldn't surprise me.

Once the landlord had decided that I wasn't really stupid (or dangerous), but merely a misguided American, we got along fine. I spent the next while sitting at the picnic table outside where I adjusted my watch to reflect local time and wrote up a few notes. On the stroke of 12, I went back in to the bar, was greeted cordially, drank one or two pints and ate the most extraordinarily wonderful beef pie and chips.

The climb from Machen, over Mynydd Machen and down to Crosskeys was a bit of a slog, especially since my body was trying to adjust to its new diet of alcohol and lard. By the time I reached the summit the clouds had rolled in and a stiff breeze had sprung up. I had brought various layers of weather protection with me and this only warranted my first line of defence - a wind-proof, breathable $1 Tyvec bio-hazard jacket. This incredibly light, if somewhat peculiar garment worked wonderfully, keeping me warm and dry.

The valleys of this part of Wales are heavily developed, and the Ebbw Vale is no exception. Fortunately, the surrounding hills are not, and I was lucky enough to have them to my self for the day. Twmbarlwm mountain, or the 'nipple' or 'pimple' as it is affectionately known, is crowned with a substantial Iron Age hill fort with a Norman Motte and Bailey Castle at one end. There are supposed to be outstanding views of the surrounding countryside promised on the rare days when the sky is clear. I suppose the low cloud I enjoyed was the price for having it to myself.

By mid afternoon, jet lag was starting to catch up with me and I was feeling dead tired as I headed north-east along the ridge beyond the fort. Some might uncharitably argue that it might have been the lunch time beer weighing me down, but either way, I began to look for a place to camp as the weather turned cool, damp and breezy. Whether I was too tired to pay attention, or whether the mist and slope of the ground obscured it, I don't know, but I ended up camping just on the outskirts of the new town of Cwmbran without realizing it. I had hopped over a stone wall, found a more or less level spot for my bivvy in a small woods and spent a quiet and comfortable night before I ever noticed that the adjacent town extended almost all the way up the hillside to where I stayed.

My first inkling that I wasn't too far removed from civilization came early the next morning. I had just answered the call of nature and had barely hoisted up my pants when a tweedy woman with two black Labradors walked briskly past. One of the dogs showed altogether too much interest in the patch of moor I had just that moment vacated and had to be chivvied away. Mental note to self: conduct ablutions in a more secluded spot if you can find one!

The next day was one long, tiring, glorious ridge walk. The first half involved a gradual climb up to the summit of Mynydd Maen and a long slow descent into Pontypool. My route skirted the town but not the road re-alignment works which were under construction when I arrived. I had to get to the other side of the A472 interchange, but it was closed. I was on the verge of getting frustrated when a group of teenage lads came along. They willingly led me through a mess of back lanes and underpasses until I was safely on the other side - thanks lads!

My meagre food stocks had diminished to virtually nothing so I stopped at a gas (petrol) station / convenience store to replenish with such health food items as pre-packaged sausage rolls, chocolate milk, hobnob biscuits, blackcurrant pop and Mars bars. I sat on my pack sheltering from the rain while I decanted the pop from its floppy plastic bottle into my aluminium water bottles and ogled the selection of diesel passenger vans in the dealership across the road.

A broad path leads through the ornate gates of Pontypool Park, through the park and onwards towards the Pontypool Folly - a prominent local landmark with an interesting history. It was originally built between 1765 and 1770 by John Hanbury (who also built Pontypool Park), as a summer house and renovated in the 1830's by Capel Hanbury Leigh. Throughout the nineteenth and early twentieth centuries, it was a favourite local picnic spot. During the second world war, someone had the bright idea that this landmark might assist the Luftwaffe in locating a local Ordnance Factory, so acting under the Emergency Powers (Defence) Act of 1939, it was demolished. Immediately following the war, attempts were made to raise enough money to rebuild it. Finally, the rebuild was completed in 1994 and the tower was re-opened by HRH Prince of Wales in a formal ceremony.

Although the commanding views from near the tower were delightful, I found myself far more interested in the two ancient gentlemen who, along with their equally ancient dogs, were making their way up the approach hill. At a stile, the dogs took the opportunity to sniff my legs while we all caught our breath. They had just come out from Pontypool to catch a bit of fresh air, they said.

A series of minor farm tracks finally dwindled into a high path along the ridge which parallels the Llywd valley. The uplands in this area are part of the Brecon Beacons National Park. I always associate national parks with hoards of day hikers, but to my great pleasure, I had the ridge to myself and didn't see another person until I reached Abergavenny.

The ridge walk includes a number of trig points, most of which don't warrant map names but which include Garn Wen (425m), and Blorenge (552m.) the highest of all. Each trig point is like a personal milestone. You slog up the slope to the concrete pillar, throw your rucksack off and spend a few minutes relishing the quiet, the view and the mini-achievement of the climb. My camera allows me to capture a little bit of sound with each photograph, and I was getting in to the habit of recording a short description with each shot. My entry for the summit of Garn Wen consists of a long happy sigh followed by "just me and the skylarks".

The descent from Blorenge to Abergavenny was brutal. My legs felt like jelly and my feet were starting to ache. So far, I had avoided blisters by changing my socks frequently, and giving my feet a chance to air every time I stopped for a break. Nevertheless, until they got used to the new demands being made of them, my feet expressed their discontent quite vociferously.

I had thought of finding a B&B in Abergavenny, or at the very least a decent supper in a pub. In the end I did neither. After buying some provisions at a grocery store, and wasting some time getting lost in more suburbs, I stumbled out of town heading generally north along a minor road in the darkening evening. When I was younger I used to start looking for a place to stay fairly early in the day. The idea that I might be caught out at night without having my accommodation properly organized used to terrify me. Things have changed. Now I know that there will always be somewhere to put your head down. It may not be comfortable, scenic or nice - but it will do.

In the end, the road dwindled to a path which broke into pieces threading through a mature woods as a series of cattle trails. By this time I had walked far further than I had intended, and it was almost dark. Finally I found a more-or-less flat section of the path, strung up my bivvy, levelled out the ground as best I could with my pack and extra clothes, and quickly fell asleep.

Lord Hereford's Knob

Although by now it may seem as though I was ambling aimlessly through the Welsh countryside, I was actually attempting to follow an unofficial long distance path called the Cambrian Way, devised by Tony Drake in the late nineteen sixties. At one time there had been a hope that Tony's route or some variation thereof, would be adopted as a National Trail but for various reasons, all too tedious and bureaucratic to itemize here, this has never happened. The Cambrian Way remains as a loose connection of public footpaths and natural routes from Cardiff to Conway which takes in most of the highest parts of the landscape. Unlike the National Trails, it's poorly known and rarely used - just the way I like it. One can elect to follow Tony's excellent guide book, or navigate your own way. I was already starting to diverge. My exit from Abergavenny had fortuitously led me away from Tony's route and into the nicely secluded woods. Had I stuck strictly to his recommended path I would have had to spend the night on the windswept uplands and would have missed out on a delightful night on my soggy bit of cow path.

The new day dawned misty and still. The climb up to the Sugar Loaf was a steady trudge with no views, no company, not even a sheep bleating in the mist. I didn't linger long on the summit as the air was damp and chilly, but quickly descended on boulder strewn slopes to small roads along Grwyne Fawr and the path north to the Black Mountains. Many years ago, I'd cycled some of the minor roads in the Black Mountains and Brecon Beacons area, but I'd never tramped them on foot and was eager for the chance. Fortunately the earlier mist was evaporating, the sun was visible again, and while it never actually became warm, at least it was clear.

As far as I was concerned, the big cylindrical cairn on the top of Garnwen marked the southern end of the mountains. Whether this is technically correct, I have no idea - that's just how it felt to me. I'd hardly had a chance to sling my pack down and get out the camera when a group of women arrived, opened their packs and started what was evidently going to be a lengthy lunch. Rather than intrude on their solitude - no, I'll rephrase that - since they had intruded on my solitude, I opted to continue down the well trodden path north to the next trig point at Bal Mawr, where, fortunately, there was no one else around. It's not that I'm anti-social of course: I just like being on my own.

Generations of feet have worn a deep groove in the top of the Black Mountains. On a clear day, you can see it snaking across the landscape for miles. I'm sure it's a nightmare for those responsible for erosion control, as all the bracken and heather has long since been worn away, revealing a broad swath of hard packed mud and rocks, but it makes for some easy walking. At this point I was doing well. I had settled into an easy stride, my pack didn't feel too heavy and my legs were holding up. Only a slight, niggling awareness of my feet was starting to work its way into my consciousness.

I followed that snaking path for about eleven miles over Waun Fach and Rhiw y Fan to Lord Hereford's Knob. I'm sure there's a joke there but I can't, for the life of me, think what it might be. Along the way, my feet decided that they'd had quite enough of this rough treatment and had begun to sing to me. At first I ignored them. I had no chafing or blisters, just a dull, but gradually increasing ache. By the time I got to Lord Hereford's the ache had become a rather insistent demand that I stop, take my boots off and allow the poor dears a chance to expand in the fresh air.

I found a really nice rocky outcrop overlooking the valley below. A lovely expanse of pastoral countryside was spread out between my crinkly and aching feet but I couldn't quite see Hay-on-Wye - my destination for the evening. Those last few miles to Hay were a bit of a struggle. My feet felt like blocks of concrete; they'd long ago given up trying to flex or conform to the movement of my boots, and let me know about it with every footfall. Once I hit the roads, each foot step jarred and hurt. This wasn't fun any more.

At Hay-on-Wye, I stayed at the first B&B I could find, close to the centre of town. I was expecting a high price and was pleasantly surprised to get a good room with a massive bathtub for far less than I expected. After soaking in the tub for a while, I hobbled down the road for some fish and chips and a pint or two. There must have been something magical in that beer because in the morning, my feet felt perfect again and all pain was gone.

It always seems to take the first few days of a long hike for the body to adjust. After the first day, you are usually exhausted, especially if your body is also trying to get its circadian rhythms aligned. Day two and sometimes day three are for pain. Muscles ache, feet get sore and blistered, pack straps dig in; making progress is like walking through molasses. Then magically, somewhere around day four, its as if the body concedes that it has to adjust to the new regime, capitulates and just gets on with it. You find you are just walking. Not walking thinking about your feet, or walking thinking about the weight of the pack - just walking. The miles roll by and at the end of the day, you're just tired, not exhausted, not aching, just nicely, happily tired.

No Pub at Storey Arms

Even though I was feeling good, it was a bit irritating to have to back-track along the same roads to get back to the uplands again, but since I had promised myself a night in Hay-on-Wye, that was the price. Time has a wonderful tendency to erase unpleasant memories and crystallize the good parts; my recollection of the long ridge walk south to Crickhowell is one of a healthy body, extensive views, a sense of elevation and the odd skylark. As you may have gathered already, I'm partial to skylarks; they sing of open moors and clear spring days. They are one of the many things I miss.

I had deviated from the main path south, at the summit of Waun

Fach. Instead of bearing slightly to the west, following the main upland ridge, I headed due south, skirting the headwaters of a small stream and ending up at the edge of a sizeable belt of woodland, enclosed by a stone wall. Something shiny white caught my eye near the bank of a rivulet. I dropped my pack and went over to investigate.

The white object was a canine lower jaw; the scattered remains of the animal were close by. I looked at the jaws and skull a little more closely. The ants and flies had done their work. There wasn't a scrap of flesh or fur to be seen. A fox? Was it shot? I looked for any obvious signs of trauma or shell fragments, but there was nothing to help me flesh out my understanding of the scene. I left the bones to bleach in the sun, but have carried the memory of them with me for a long time.

Crickhowell was such a logical place to stay that I unbuckled my wallet again and spent a second night in a B&B. Actually I was bushwhacked. I was aimlessly wandering down the street when a fellow walking his dog on the other side of the road shouted across:

"Are you looking for a Bed & Breakfast?". I admitted I was, even though the idea hadn't really fully formed by that time.

"Just carry on until you see the sign and walk in. I'll be along in a minute".

I found the B&B without any trouble and had barely enough time to shed my pack and my boots when the owner returned. His dog - a scruffy little border collie - immediately pounced on me. Since I live in a world of dog slobber and hair, I imagine that to other dogs I'm instantly recognizable as a receptive target for their affections. They're usually right! The poor owner was concerned that I would be annoyed and immediately hustled the dog behind a half-door where it whined and scrabbled pitifully. He needn't have bothered; my dog slobber quotient needed replenishing.

My little room was warm and comfortable, but, I suspect, a far cry from the elegance offered by the Dragon Hotel, which had caught my eye as I was leaving town. The building is in two halves: a large, lime-yellow Georgian front half faces on to one street, while a lower, longer wing clad in subtle pink plaster, extends along the High Street. Although it too has been somewhat Georgianized, it is clearly the older part of the hotel. Their literature suggests 16th century: I'm inclined to believe them.

Leaving Crickhowell by the famous 18th century bridge across the River Usk, it didn't take long before I was near water again, following the tow-path of the Monmouth and Brecon canal for a few kilometres. Walking canal tow-paths is easy going. The terrain is flat, the paths are usually well worn, and the early industrial scenery is strangely restful. I spent a happy few moments on a canal-side bench adjusting my boots before heading back into the hills. During my teenage years I had spent a lot of time along canal footpaths. I used to fish, or more accurately, I used to sit on the canal bank for hours watching a float bobbing in the water, in the hope that something might, one day, decide to take my bait. It never bothered me much whether I caught anything or not, which is a good thing because I rarely did. I was just as content to sit quietly. I learned early on that if I could sit still, eventually the nearby birds and animals would start to view me as part of the landscape and carry on with what they were doing before I interrupted them. Seeing a water vole bumbling about his business, completely unaware of my existence was a great source of pleasure for me.

Beyond Llangattock my path climbed abruptly up an old mine tramway to the base of a long series of crags. On a sunny day, this area is spectacular, with great views of Crickhowell and the valley of the River Usk to one side and steep, bluffs and cliffs to the other. I paused briefly to catch my breath after the long climb, then ploughed on.

For the next hour or two I was in heaven. The weather was mild and clear and the walking was across high, level moorland, along a clear, but not overly damage path. I crossed a small road then headed west towards the 'Chartist Cave' marked on the OS map. Although it lies only about a mile from the nearest road, the Chartist Cave - yes, it's a real cave - feels remote and a bit secret. Apparently, disaffected workers seeking political reform stockpiled weapons and gathered there before marching against government forces in Newport. Guess how well that went!

I'm good at walking. I can cover distance well, I am fairly tireless, don't suffer much with sore body parts and never get bored with my own company but I am a lousy quartermaster. I never buy enough food, and what I do buy hardly counts as food as far as most people are concerned. I never carry pots and pans or any cooking equipment. If I managed to remember to go into a grocery shop at all, I'm likely to emerge with half a dozen chocolate bars, some biscuits and some pop. If I'm really on the ball I might remember to grab a malt loaf or a fruit cake - something with a high calorie to weight ratio - but it's always touch and go. This incompetence gradually became a bit of an issue. Naively, I was working on the assumption that where the map said 'PH' there would be a pub, and wherever a village was shown, there might be a shop. Silly me. It hadn't sunk in yet that Britain had changed since I roamed these hills. The car now ruled everything. Big stores in the major towns had all the trade; the village shop was more-or-less dead.

After about another mile, I came upon a small car park, close to a scenic waterfall. Nobody was around so I spent a few minutes having another short break. I allowed myself half a Mars Bar, a couple of biscuits and a swig of blackberry juice. I knew I would have to eke out my remaining food for at least a couple of days. I wasn't likely to be able to re-provision until Llandovery. As evening was approaching, I started looking for somewhere to camp. The sun sets by about 7PM in late March and I wanted to get set up so that I wouldn't be stumbling around in the dark.

Perhaps I should explain my accommodation. In planning for this trip, I decided that I wanted to keep weight to a minimum. I wanted each piece of my equipment to perform as many tasks as possible, so.....my rain gear was also my tent. I had brought two military rain ponchos; the kind that can be snapped together edge to edge. They were light and worked perfectly well as rain coats, as long as you tucked in the excess material so that it didn't flap in the wind. They also made an excellent tent. I had brought some light metal tent pegs and some parachute cord. With those, and my hiking poles, I was able to make a perfect little solo 'A' shaped tent. I didn't bother with a ground sheet. My self-inflating (military again) sleeping pad was completely waterproof. Once inside there wasn't much room for moving around, but I was there to sleep, not do gymnastics. As long as it was properly pegged and the poles were sunk well into the ground, I was warm and dry all night. Best of all, since the ponchos were camo pattern and the whole structure was low to the ground, it became virtually invisible. Stealth camping at its best! Two ponies watched me as I erected my shelter but stayed well out of petting reach. I wonder what they thought of the new element on their landscape.

11 hours between dust and dawn can be along time. I am usually up and moving as soon as there is any light in the sky, but this time I lingered until some of the mist had cleared and the sun was well and truly up. I was looking forward to this day. I would be spending almost all day walking along part of the Beacons Way; a long ridge walk all the way to Pen-y-Fan then down to Storey Arms.

It turned out to be a magnificent day. I clambered up the trail next to a waterfall and on to the first ridge. The mist was still hanging in the valleys, but the tops of all the hills were bathed in hazy sunlight. The gently sloping backs of the hills lie to the south-west. On the north-east side, the land falls abruptly away into a group of deep, U-shaped glacial valleys. It was superb walking and I had it entirely to myself until I reached Pen-y-Fan where a few day-hikers had struggled up from their cars below. Pen-y-Fan is the highest mountain in south Wales. Not surprisingly, it attracts quite a few people. I didn't mind though; it was nice to see some people for a change.

I don't envy anyone the climb up to Pen-y-Fan from the car park at Storey Arms. It's a brutal, unremitting 1200 foot slog, up a slope that seems to go on for ever. I was lucky; I was coming down and gravity was with me. Not so for the small group of teenagers and their leader - let's call him Mike - who were making their way to the summit. They had stopped by the path and were sitting dejectedly in the thick heather. Mike was having a hard time motivating them to keep climbing.

I must have been looking a bit weather-worn, and with my big pack and scruffy grey beard, more like a hobo than a hiker. I expect it was immediately obvious that I wasn't just out for the day. They asked me where I was going. They looked shocked when I told them Conway. They asked me where I was coming from. They were even more shocked to hear Cardiff. I'm not sure they entirely believed me. Lastly, Mike asked me where I was going to stay that night. They seemed shocked again when I said I had no idea and that I'd just find somewhere to bivvy but was heading in the general direction of Llandovery.

We chatted for a while and I did my best to inspire them with helpful things like: 'just keep putting one foot in front of the other', 'don't be afraid to take breathers and you'll soon be up'. I have no idea whether my advise had any effect. When I turned around to look they were no longer visible, presumably hidden in one of the hollows and obscured from my view.

I had foolishly thought that there might be a pub at Storey Arms but if there ever was, there certainly isn't now. There was a burger van though, so I was able to fill up with a burger and a big cup of coffee before heading due west across Fforest Fawr, ultimately heading for Llyn-y-Fan Fawr, a pretty little lake at the foot of one of the highest mountains in the region. But first, I had many miles to go over rough hill and moor. Using the timer on my camera, I took a photograph of my self standing on the path. I'm wearing shorts so my skinny legs are visible. My shirt is unbuttoned and my belly is overwhelming my belt. It's not a pretty picture, but I look content. I was, and anyway, with my haphazard approach to provisions, my belly was disappearing rapidly.

Tony Drake's route was designed it to take in the maximum number of hilltops. His guide book jacket describes it as "A Tough High Level Coast to Coast Walk through Wildest Wales". During the 275 miles from start to finish, the vertical ascent is about 61,540 feet – or about twice the height of Everest, so you won't be surprised to hear that his route drags you up virtually every bump on the map until you're heartily sick of trig points. On the plus side, I share his obvious delight in eschewing formal paths in favour of just heading straight across the uplands. The next day promised plenty of such unconstrained walking.

That night I had a rather unusual camp. Instead of using my ponchos to make a tent, I made a simple lean-to against a stone wall, holding the upper edge down with rocks and pegging the lower edge. By tying my strings to the hood of each poncho, and attaching the strings to my poles, I managed to create plenty of usable space. The ends were open to the weather, but it didn't look as though a deluge was likely. It wasn't the most elegant shelter I have ever created. The ground against the base of the wall was, to put it mildly, a bit lumpy, but I survived the night, so it must have been OK.

Considering that it was only late March, I was enjoying spectacular weather; warm and sunny during the day, with minimal breeze, cool and comfortable at night. When anticipating hiking in Wales, a wise man expects rain. For once I was both wise and lucky.

Damsels and Hags

The morning started off a bit hazy, as if foreboding some change in the weather. I was soon decamped and heading roughly north-east in the general direction of Llyn y Fan Fawr, past a rather nice prehistoric stone circle. For some reason, I had it in my mind that Llyn y Fan Fawr was associated with the Arthurian legend of the 'Lady of the Lake', but I was wrong on all counts. In subsequent reading, I discovered that the Arthurian legend is associated with a whole string of different places, none of which were nearby. Moreover, while there is a local legend about a Lady and a lake, it connects to Llyn y Fan Fach – about two miles further to the west. It's a good thing I didn't waste any time waiting for my ethereal, and no doubt scantily clad damsel to appear. The lake didn't seem to be more than a few inches deep. You'd have a hard time getting your knees wet, let alone hiding a full sized damsel. Still, it's a pretty little lake, backing on to steep, rocky slopes which extend for about two miles and culminate at the crest of Fan Brycheiniog, at 2631 feet, the highest hill for miles around.

Beyond the lake, I entered a world of peat hags. No, these aren't the damsels from the lake who have grown old, but are still hanging around trying to snare an unwary mate. They are the eroding edges of upland peat bogs. Peat forms on uplands when wet, dead vegetation builds up over time – lots of it. Lack of oxygen in the wet environment prevents the plant remains from decaying fully, so they gradually accumulate as thick layers of peat, capped by actively growing moorland plants. When erosion occurs around the edges of the bogs, the peat is exposed and gets undercut, leaving the active vegetation sitting on top like a hat. As I entered this somewhat eerie landscape, I could see a thick bank of mist lying in the direction I would be walking. Soon it was all around me and visibility was down to a few feet.

I have quite a few things to thank my grammar school for: a certain tolerance of pain from years of corporal punishment, a well developed capacity to withstand cold and wet from years of playing rugby every Friday afternoon whatever the weather, and an ability to read a map and use a compass. We had a visionary headmaster who, long before such things were in vogue, bought a unused one room school in central Wales and converted it into 'The Mountain Centre'. The fortunate, or in my case, the eager, were allowed to go and do week long field study trips, which mostly involved long days hiking in the Berwyn Mountains, during which the teacher might casually say, 'that's a U-shaped valley' or 'see that lateral moraine'. Part of the deal was that we shouldn't get lost. Using a map and compass became second nature.

Darn good thing too! The mist had come down so thickly that if I turned around twice, I wouldn't have had any idea which direction I was going, or from which direction I had come. With trusty map and compass, I set a bearing for the north-west corner of a Roman Camp which lay about 2 miles away, where the road from Trecastle crossed my route.

Following a compass bearing when you can hardly see a few feet in front of you is an exercise in faith. You have to learn to 'trust the force', since your mind will try to convince you that you are going in completely the wrong direction, and the landscape will try to divert you with unexpected obstacles and paths which look as though they will make life so much easier if only you follow them. You have to steel your mind, trust the compass, check it every few steps, and just have faith. I did, and, with a big, self congratulatory smirk on my face, I can tell you I came out within a few feet of where I was aiming.

By the time I passed the end of the Usk Reservoir, a breeze had come up and the mist was starting to dissipate. Within a couple of miles, I hit another small road and from there until Llandovery, four miles further on I was walking on the road.

After walking on the uneven moorland surface for hours, the first few hundred yards on a paved road feel marvellous and amazingly fast. No longer do you have to watch where to place every foot so as to avoid rocks, stumps and bog. You can just settle into a steady rhythm and make good time. For the first few hundred yards! After that, the steady rhythm starts to get monotonous and the hard road makes your feet hurt. All those little micro-adjustments necessary for each step on the rough ground have actually been keeping you from getting sore and tired. Suddenly I was conscious of my pack. I could feel warmth starting to build up under the ball of my foot, my thighs started to ache. Darn it – I hate walking on roads.

I had already decided that I would look for a pub or a B&B in Llandovery, but as soon as I saw the Castle Hotel, I knew it was for me and to heck with the expense. It was a little posh for a sweat soaked and peat stained hiker, so I wasn't too surprised to be shown to a little garret room in the back corner of the uppermost floor. It was little more than a modified broom cupboard but I didn't care. It was clean and there was plenty of hot water, a comfortable bed and a TV. Sometimes simple pleasures, well earned, are the best.

I had no intentions of blowing any more of my budget on fancy food in the hotel though, so as soon as I was clean and decent again, I headed back out in to the town. On my way to the hotel I had passed a fish and chip shop. I soon found it again, extravagantly opting to pay the extra to eat inside on formica and plastic.

Most of the next morning was spent walking on small, winding roads and farm tracks with the occasional traverse across a few fields for good measure. The route roughly paralleled the valley of the Towy, and would continue to do so for quite a few miles. Although it was early in the day, I was ready for a pint by the time I reached Rhandirmwyn. The Royal Oak pub, and much of the village, sits on the edge of the valley, but I eschewed the view from the tables outside for a place at the bar and a quick conversation with the owner over a pint and a bag of crisps.

After the pub, the day just got better and better as the small road I was following changed in to a farm track and eventually continued as a footpath up the side of a small stream. The valley bottoms were a mixture of sheep pasture and woods while the surrounding hill tops were rough heather, bracken and rock outcrops. As I headed up the valley, the walls of the pass closed in until the path was little more than a sheep track, clinging to the slope above the stream. The weather remained glorious: warm enough to be pleasant, cool enough that despite the exertion, I didn't turn into a sweat sodden mess.

After a few miles the stream bifurcated. Right at the junction of the two arms, I noticed a level terrace and the overgrown foundation of a small cottage or field barn. Even though it was early in the day, it was such a delightful spot that I decided to stay. After erecting my bivvy, I spent happy hours listening to the sounds of the bubbling water, watching a Dipper diving in and out of the pools, as the sun gradually sank behind the hills.

I was still moving well. By lunchtime I had hiked over the hill into the valley of the River Camddwr, passed the delightful Calvanist Chapel at Soar Mynydd – reputedly the most remote in Wales - and followed the tiny road north until it petered out at the Nantymaen farm. Beyond the farm, I was back into a quiet world of mist, hills and sheep. The sun gradually broke the mist just before I arrived at Strata Florida, the ruined 12th century Cistercian Abbey which once dominated much of central Wales. Now, only the Great West Door to the Abbey Church remains standing. Most of the other walls are little more than head height.

There was no one about to extract an entrance fee, so I dumped my rucksack near the gate and wandered around alone. It was a peaceful place to spend a few moments. I could feel a bit of melancholy starting to descend on me, so the opportunity to sit on a bench for a while and revive my flagging spirits with a chocolate bar and a drink was most welcome. From the map, I could see that the village of Pontrhydfenigaid was just a mile to the west. Once again, those magic letters 'PH' drew me like moth to a flame.

The only B&B in the village was closed, but the owner opened for me anyway. As I lay on the bed, her husband started playing the guitar, quite well, in the room below. Sadly, he was soon told to stop – I'm assuming on the pretext that it might be disturbing me – but nothing could have been further from the truth. With the evenings entertainment over, I walked down to the pub for a supper and a couple of pints.

"Good evening sir. What can I get you?"

"I'd like a pint of..............(I can no longer remember what was on offer) please"

"What part of the States are you from?"

"Actually, I'm English, but I've been living in Canada for nearly forty years. I must have picked up a bit of an accent."

While he poured my beer and I waited for the gammon and eggs I'd ordered, we had short chat about living in Canada, and a much long one about merits and qualities of German Shepherd dogs. We were both missing ours.

Second meeting

Rather than retrace my steps to Strata Florida, I took a minor road north-east from my B&B, rejoining the 'official' route just north of Llyn Teifi, one of the small lakes which dot this part of Wales. I was feeling fresh, the weather was mild and the landscape was open and bare, feeling surprisingly wild and desolate. There was no path to follow – the guide book provided some general guidelines and directions towards Devil's Bridge across open moorland. This was hiking at it's best.

How I avoided the Hotel bar in Devil's Bridge I can no longer recall, but I resupplied at a small shop then headed west along the narrow gauge railway which hugs the side of the steeply wooded valley. After less than a mile, I crossed the Afon Rheidol then started the laborious clamber up the steep slope on the other side of the valley, past numerous old mine workings from the silver, lead and zinc operations which had turned the river into one of the most polluted in Wales. I'm glad I didn't know that at the time, as I'm inclined to take a sip from just about any flowing water I pass, as long as it looks wholesome.

Although it was only the last day of March, that afternoon was hot. By the time I'd got out of the valley I was ready to stop for the day and was in no mood to look for somewhere to bivvy. Fortuitously, the path led almost straight to the door of the George Burrow Hotel, a 17th century Inn possibly once frequented by the famous hiker and author after whom it's named. My room was ordinary, but clean, large and close to the bar.

I had paid for the room in advance, so in the morning I just got up and left. Much later in the day that I realised I had walked off with the room key. In the meantime I had a date with Plynlimon – the highest mountain in central Wales and the source of the Severn, Dee and Rheidol Rivers.

As the elevation increased, so did the wind. By the time I was at the Dyll Faen woods it had risen enough that the whole edge of the plantation was in motion as if it was alive. What am I saying? Of course it was alive, but the wind made it seem animate. Beyond the woods was a steady climb to the cairn at the summit and the full force of the blustery wind. The light nylon fabric of my trousers began to flap wildly, in danger of tearing themselves apart. I was only just able to keep my footing while I snapped the inevitable picture of the trig point and the misty hills beyond and started my descent. Once again, it seemed as though I had the whole of central Wales to myself. There was no-one on Plylimon, and no-one visible on the surrounding hills. I saw nobody until later the following day. That night I camped against a wire fence between a forestry commission plantation and the open moor. It wasn't my best bivvy ever, but it provided some shelter from the persistent wind, and as usual, I slept well.

After about a mile of easy, early morning hill walking, I missed the path and took a detour away from the route described in Tony Drake's guide, following a series of farm tracks and minor roads down into the valley of the River Dovey. I was just as happy with this detour. The prescribed route follows a footpath along the ridge which parallels the river. The ridge is plastered with wind turbines which held no fascination for me: I took the low road.

I was making good progress along the road to Aberangell, my sticks clattering with each step as I picked up the pace, when the first car I'd seen all day drew along-side.

"Hello there. Did you make it to Llandovery that day?"

I must have looked a little stunned. I had no idea who this well dressed person was, who seemed to know all about me.

"I was leading the group of school children. We met you on Pen-Y-Fan"

Six days had passed since I'd met them. Without the hiking gear and the kids in tow, I hadn't recognized Mike. I told him I'd decided to bivvy on the hillside a few miles from where we'd met, then carried on the Llandovery the next day.

We chatted for a while about how the kids had managed the climb. I was pleased to hear that despite the whining, they had all made it to the top and had ended the day feeling pleased with themselves.

"Are you still heading to Conway?"

I thought this question was a bit odd since I was well north of where I had originally met them and obviously making good progress. Then I realised it was for the benefit of the person in the passenger seat who, of course, hadn't got a clue why the driver was talking to a tramp at the side of the road.

I assured him I was indeed still heading for Conway, and was looking forward to the more rugged terrain of Snowdonia before reaching the coast. I like to think that the kids I'd met on Pen-Y-Fan were pleased and impressed when he told them of my progress, but I suspect they just thought, 'Daft old codger!'

Another good piece of news did come from our conversation; the pub at Mallwyd, just a mile or two up the road, was open and I was well overdue for a pint.

The Brigands Inn is an imposing 15th century coaching inn, right at the intersection of the roads to Dolgellau, Welshpool and Machynlleth which exuded the sense that it has been cornering the market on accommodation, food and refreshment for a long, long time. It looked a bit up scale for the likes of me – or my liking for that matter – but I brushed past the Range Rovers and BMWs in the parking lot, dumped my rucksack over the low wall by the entrance and marched into the bar. At the time, I must have been fixated on that pint. Usually I'm rather interested in old buildings, but I simply didn't notice the beams and the flagstone floors until I looked at some pictures just now. The drink went down well though, I was treated with an acceptable level of civility, and was in good humour when I stepped back out into the sunshine an hour later, heavier in the bladder and lighter in the pocket.

By crossing the river and sticking to minor roads then forestry tracks, I bypassed Dinas Mawddwy, taking a path which led high up on to the ridge above Craig Maesglase. This is an area where ice age glaciers have cut enormous divots in the landscape. One side of the hill is rounded and smooth, the other looks as though it's been removed with an ice-cream scoop, leaving steep cliffs right below the crest.

I found a section of wire fence just above the cliffs, strung my bivvy and spent a quiet night.

Into the Slough

I had been looking forward to the next day. The walking promised to be spectacular; a long curving ridge walk, high above the surrounding valleys, with long view of the mountains to the north as long as the mist allowed. Some time in the night though, a gloom had descended on me. For the last couple of weeks I had managed to park all my anxieties about home, relationship and work. Now they all came rushing to the forefront, occupying my thoughts and making my walking sluggish. My rucksack felt twice it's normal weight, my legs felt weak, my ambition was gone.

Instead of heading toward the heights of Cribin Fawr and Waunoer, I mistakenly turned in to a steep sided valley which started leading me in the right direction, then abruptly turned south, taking me further and further from where I needed to go. In the process, I lost a lot of elevation. I had no alternative but to climb up the side of the valley, regain the ridge, then get back on my original route. The side of the valley was covered in a thick plantation and I ended up following a compass bearing, fighting my way on my hands and knees through dense forest up a 45 degree slope. By the time I was back on track, I was exhausted, hot, sweaty and miserable.

My original plan had been to drop down to the A487 south of Dolgellau, climb up on to Cadair Idris, then follow the ridge west to Arthog and the bridge across to Barmouth. When I got to the road and looked up at the climb on the other side, my heart sank. I knew it would be a hard, 12 mile slog to get to Barmouth across the mountain. On any other day I would have just gritted my teeth and got on with it. On this day, I just didn't have it in me.

As I slowly walked down the road towards the hotel at Minfford, I justified my decision in a host of different ways. I had climbed Cadair Idris many times before. I had no provisions, no water, I needed a pint and so on, but the truth was, I had lost any sense of why I was walking and had no energy at all.

I think I would have wept if the hotel had been closed – for all the good that would have done – but fortunately, it was open, even if I was the only customer. The landlord brought me a pint, set to work thawing a curry then checked the bus time tables for me. A bus to Barmouth would pass right by the hotel within the hour, giving me just enough time to eat my meal and gulp down a second pint.

Barmouth is a thin strip of a town, sandwiched between hills and the sea. I walked along the High Street, past the main shopping area, the banks, the takeaways and the shops selling seaside tat or offering caravan repairs, and on to King's Crescent with its row of narrow, 3 storey stone houses lining the east side of the street. The B&B I ended up in was classic British seaside – a bit seedy, but clean and cheap. I dropped my rucksack on the floor and lay on the bed staring at the ceiling.

I must have dozed off, but awoke to the sound of bed springs being violently exercised in the room above. As I had checked in I had overheard something about newly-weds. This was the icing on my cake of misery. Perhaps food and drink would help me to claw back from the pit. I wandered back down the road and bought a few cans of beer at the Spar and some fish and chips from the 'Dolphin' before heading slowly back to my room. The couple above must have been catching their breath because the bonking had stopped for a while and I was able to sink further into my pit without their energetic love-making distracting me.

Like most people, I have had my ups and downs from time to time. I felt disconnected from my wife and family, walking further seemed pointless, even the beer seemed flat and tasteless. I was completely lost.

Back on Top

What a difference a day makes! I awoke to bright sun streaking in through the window. They were at it again upstairs, but I couldn't have cared less. During the night I had somehow clambered from my pit. I felt full of energy, hope and focus. Avoiding what would undoubtedly have been a greasy breakfast of fishy bacon and limp eggs, I packed my gear and headed back to the Spar for some provisions, gulping down a quick breakfast of chocolate milk and biscuits while I walked.

The path north climbed quickly from the town, through bracken, gorse and rock, with widening views of the Barmouth estuary and bay as the elevation increased. Parts of the mountain side had been carved into small, stone walled fields; one of which had been built around a large boulder wearing a thick crown of vegetation like Don King's crazy hair.

This absurd thought vaporised any last lingering shreds of melancholy. When I reached the first trig point, I set my camera up in my hiking pole and took a self-portrait. I look happy, relaxed and ready for anything. I was.

The hike to the Rhinogs was a long, high level walk over rounded hills studded with rock, scree and talus. Although I had hiked in north Wales before, I had never been on the Rhinogs, whose reputation for wild beauty seemed to be known only to serious hill walkers. Certainly, there was nobody else out on the hills this fine April morning. The sky was clear, the views were magnificent and the air was still. Instead of hurrying along in my normal fashion, I took time to enjoy the views, rested frequently (something I barely ever do) and soaked in the quiet. I lingered on the summits of Diffwys and Y Llethr, absorbing the view of the rocky mass of Rhinog Fach across the still surface of Llyn Hywel, one of the corrie lakes which dot the mountains. I stared in amazement at the vast human effort involved in building the long dry stone wall which traverses the ridge above the lake. I had no desire to be anywhere else. This was as close to perfection as it gets.

It was shaping up to be a short day and that was fine by me. After scrambling up to the top of Rhinog Fach, I descended to the lake then followed the narrow pass towards Rhinog Fawr. As I walked I heard the screeching of Peregrine Falcons high up on the cliffs above a tiny tarn. It made me immensely happy to know they were there. They were nesting high enough up the cliff and far enough from the tarn that I didn't think my presence in the area would disturb them, so I erected my bivvy on the flats, laid out my sleeping pad and bag and settled down to watch the show as the sun threw long shadows across the water. The birds circled high above, occasionally disappearing in to the excrement streaked cliff where it was clear they had their nest. I couldn't tell whether they were feeding young yet, or just preparing the nest which, judging from the extent of the white streaks was an ancestral one. Eventually the light faded and the birds fell silent. I pulled my bedding inside the bivvy, made sure the edges were well tucked in case it rained during the night and settled in.

I woke to the sound of voices and two light beams playing over my shelter. I poked my head out between the ponchos and a voice asked,

"Is everything all right?"

I assured them that everything was just fine. The voices and lights receded and darkness settled in again. Before falling asleep, I thought about the steep path down from the summit of Glyder Fach, which had been no picnic in broad daylight. Whoever those people were, they were either crazy, skilful or perhaps both.

What was going on with Wales? Instead of the rain and wind I had anticipated, the next day brought glorious sunshine and dry, warm air. Quickly packing up my gear in the early morning light, I walked the remaining few hundred yards down into the pass between the two mountains, almost stepping on the bodies of my two night time visitors who were asleep in bivvy bags right in the middle of the path. And I thought I was into minimalist camping!

Rhinog Fawr is a massive, monolithic block of tilted, Cambrian greywacke, virtually devoid of vegetation. A few shreds of heather cling to the less precipitous terraces between the bands of eroded rock and scree which look like angled steps up the mountain side. I was anticipating a bit of a scramble, but climbing to the flat peak ended up being less testing than I had imagined. I spent a while exploring the top, taking a few photographs of the surrounding hills and dreamily peering north towards Snowdonia, just visible through the haze.

An hour or two later, as I sat having a quick break at the edge of a plantation above Lynn Trawsfynydd, my two visitors from the night before stopped for a chat. It turned out that they were outdoor adventure teachers, just out for a private hike. I had been dithering about which way to head next but they assured me that they knew of an attractive route along the south side of the stream, and of a cosy pub in Maentwrog. It didn't take much persuasion for me to join them.

Plans change when alcohol is involved. I can no longer remember what led me to the decision to catch the bus to Porthmadog that evening, but I did, found another cheap B&B and spent a comfortable night mercifully free of the sound of other peoples nocturnal exercises. In the morning, I found a bus heading for Beddgelert, a few miles up the road, and sat chatting to the driver while we waited for his appointed time to leave. It turned out that the driver had a soft spot for Canada so my ride to Beddgelert didn't cost me a penny. From there I went south along the river path, before heading inland and into the mountains again. I had been told not to miss Cnicht, a long, high ridge which, when seen from some directions, bears a passing resemblance to the Matterhorn. Yeah, right! The climb up was really just a long, steady slog, but the view was worth it. To the south, the ridge dropped precipitously to the valley below; to the north the mass of Snowdon dominated the view. What I hadn't realized until then was that this was the Saturday of the Easter weekend and the whole of Snowdonia was crawling with visitors. There must have been thirty or forty people on the summit of Cnicht, mostly sitting eating sandwiches in little groups or standing, enjoying the views. I ended up chatting to a group of young people who had driven up from London for a weekend of hiking and were enjoying their break from the big city. I like to think they were impressed that I'd walked from Cardiff, but they were probably just being polite.

Eager to leave the crowds behind, I took a direct route down from the summit, making a bee-line straight for Snowdon. This meant a rather precipitous downward scramble – I just typed scrabble, but that is equally appropriate – down the side of the ridge, over short sections of cliff, and over vegetation covered talus. At times, I had to reach far below me with my poles to find the next foot hold and to avoid toppling off the mountain. In the end though, I reached a footpath safely and carried on to Bethania and the start of the Watkin Path up Snowdon.

Not surprisingly Snowdon was crawling with people too. As the light started to fade, most were on their way down as I headed up. I followed the well defined Watkin Path for a way, then turned west then north up Allt Maenderyn and Bwlch Main. It was my intention to get close to the summit before I lost all light, so that I could be up, on top and on my way down before the Easter Sunday hoards. I set up my bivvy against a stone wall about 400 feet below the summit in the half light. It had started to chill off a little. With the bivvy completed, I wrapped myself in my camo poncho blanket, sat on a large, low rock and watched Cnicht fading in the twilight. A few stragglers made their way down the mountain, some passing within 30 feet of where I sat without noticing either me or my bivvy. I must have blended well with the surrounding rocks.

The temperature dropped during the night and I awoke to a very slight frost. I was toasty, tucked up against the wall, but eager to get moving. I shook the frost off the ponchos, jammed them into my rucksack and hit the trail again. It was a short but energetic climb to the summit. I approached the trig point just as another hiker, who had clearly had the same idea as me, arrived from the other side. We nodded, I snapped a couple of pictures, then started my descent down the Pyg Track. I had a tough day ahead of me and wanted to make the most of it.

As predicted, a steady stream of hikers was making its way up the Pyg Track. It looked more like the pictures you see of people climbing Mount Fuji than a normal British mountain scene. As I got lower down the path, each small group had to move over to let me by. I had to watch that I didn't bash anyone with my rucksack or poke them in the eye with my poles as most people were paying attention to their footing and not looking further up the path. It was a blur of faces until someone shouted, "Hey Nick".

The group from London, that I had met on Cnicht the previous day were on their way up too. We pulled off the track and had a brief chat. They were heading up Snowdon then would be driving back to London while I continued across the Glyders and the Carnedds heading for Conway. We wished each other good travels and continued on our way.

Last Days

The sky was cloudless, the air cool and clear with just a bit of haze in the distance; a beautiful day. I continued down to Pen-y-Pass, where the car park was full and more hikers were being disgorged from the Park-and-Ride bus. I didn't tarry and was soon making my way up the side of Glyder Fach. The Glyders are the central range of mountains in Snowdonia, sandwiched between Snowdon itself and the Carnedds to the north. The three main peaks, Glyder Fach, Glyder Fawr and Tryfan are all just over 3000 feet high, are precipitous and have some of the best rock climbing in the region. I wasn't interested in climbing any rocks, but I didn't mind a bit of a scramble over some of the bare, vertically tilted slabs near the summit. As with Snowdon, there were plenty of people about but the complex and jagged peak seemed to disperse them well.

The route between Glyder Fach and Tryfan, down to the Nanc Ffrancon valley, was steep, loose and a bit tricky with a full pack, but I managed to descend without injury. While on the Glyders I had met another elderly hiker who had invited me to stay at a private climbing hut near Llyn Ogwen. After a few false starts, I found the place and spent a very pleasant evening talking with the other hikers about our various adventures in the hills.

The Carneddau is the largest continuous area of upland over 2500 feet in England and Wales. Although the main peaks are rounded and without the jagged rocks of the Glyders or the prominent peak of Snowdon, they are impressive for their hunch-shouldered mass and their brutal weather. I knew how that weather could be. Back when I was 16, while hiking on the Carnedds with some school friends I had learned an important lesson about cold, wet, endurance, hypothermia and danger. We had been doing fine, making steady progress up, despite our full packs and the lashing rain, when one of our party lay down on the sopping heather and announced that he just wanted to sleep for a while.

After much fruitless cajoling, we ended up man-handling him off the mountains by the most direct route, two of us keeping him moving while the third carried two rucksacks. An age later, we reached the pub at Capel Curig. I can still remember the smell of wet wool as the warm room heated our clothing, the steam rising all around us, while Mick shivered uncontrollably.

The Carnedds are also one of the least visited part of Snowdonia.

The day started with a long haul up to the top of Carnedd Dafydd, at 3425 feet, the second highest peak in the Carnedds and the forth highest in Snowdonia. It is more impressive for its sheer hulking size than its height. The air had become a bit misty and by the time I reached the summit, I was walking just beneath the low clouds, which added a bit of atmosphere to the walk.

From Carnedd Dafydd, much of the day would be a long ridge walk over Carnedd Llewelyn (3490 feet) then a gradual descent towards Conway. Although it was still officially part the Easter weekend, most people seemed to have used Monday as their travel day. Either that or the Carnedds really are overlooked, because there were few people around, especially once I had put a few miles under my feet. Perhaps the Carnedds attract those who, like me, verge on the antisocial. The handful of people I did meet were of the nod-and-grunt type; not given to stopping or engaging in long conversations. It suited me fine.

As I walked along, relishing what I knew would be my last day in the hills I felt rather pleased with myself. My body had held up well. Other than a few twinges I had been remarkably free from aches and pains. Since Hay-on-Wye my feet had given me no trouble, and while my rucksack had always been a bit of a burden, its weight had been manageable. If someone had said "Nick, you can't stop now, you have to walk to Scotland", I would have been just as happy to comply.

I had made no plans for the night, but as I started the long slow descent towards Conway, I found myself thinking that an evening in a pub, a good meal and a soft bed would be preferable to one more night in the bivvy. Scouring the map, I saw that if I took the old Bwlch y Ddeufaen Roman Road and followed it east past a whole cluster of prehistoric monuments to the village of Rowan, if I was really, really lucky, the pub shown on the map wouldn't have been boarded up decades ago.

Maps are treacherous things. I'm sure the prehistoric standing stones, settlements and burial chambers indicated were actually there, had I chosen to look for them, but they weren't immediately obvious from the narrow track I was following and I managed to miss them all. At one of the gates I had a quick chat with a guy with two elderly greyhounds. They endured my head petting without any sign of annoyance or enthusiasm. In my dog-deprived state, just getting my hands on their fur was definitely better than nothing.

Eventually I reached the village. There was a pub. It sold beer – and food – and had a room. My day was complete.

The last day was a road walk to Conway. It was relatively quiet but otherwise not very memorable. Eventually, the castle loomed, rising up the hill from the river flats, all turrets and crenelations as a good castle should be. I passed through the town, crossed on the modern road bridge which parallels Thomas Telford's suspension road bridge (the first in the world) then headed for the Llandudno railway station on the east side of the river. I had a date at my brother's house in Birmingham – my niece was getting married in a couple of days. Hiking in Britain was over for this year.

North of Cardiff

Actually, I'm English

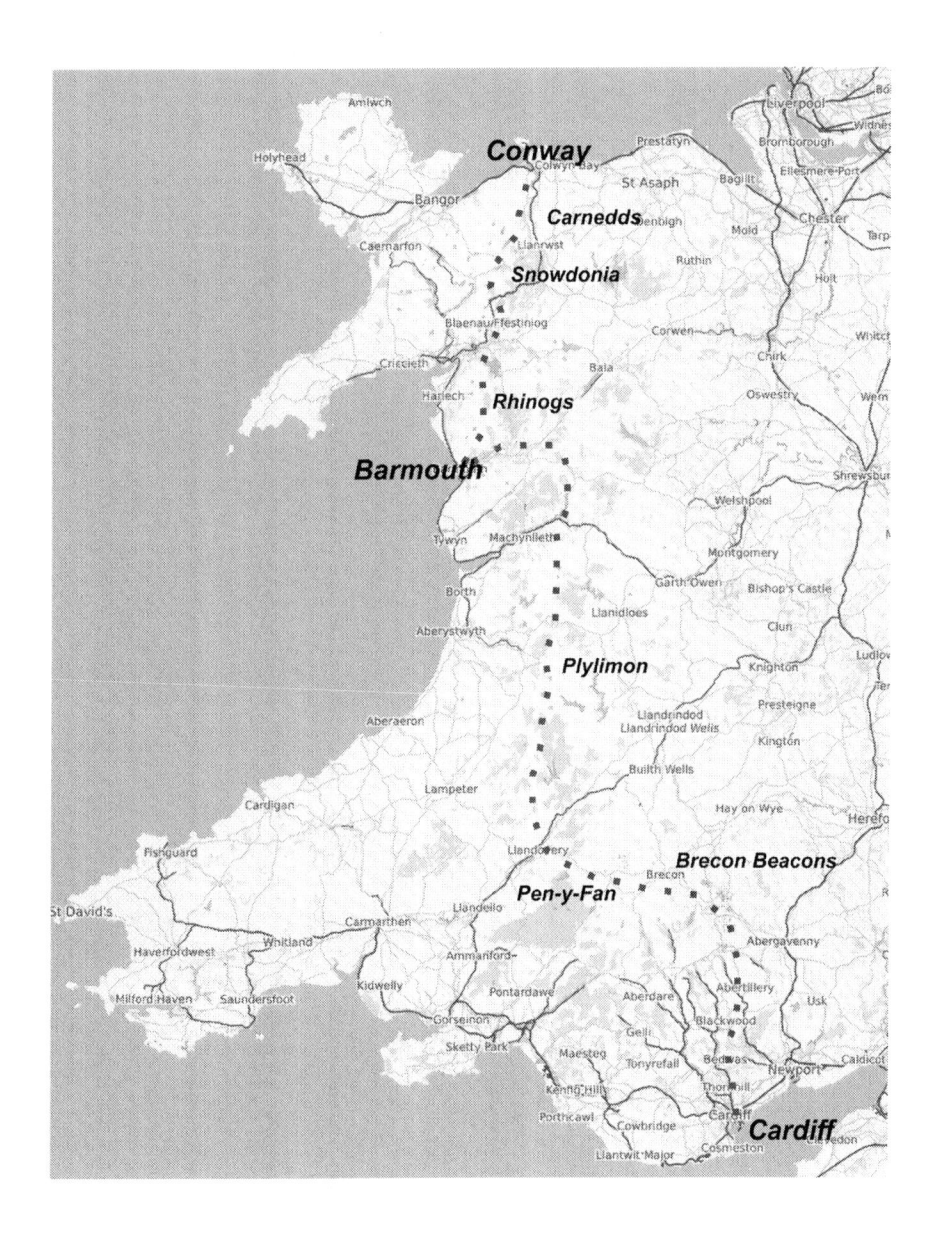

Airing my feet

Bivvy on Snowdon

PART 2

THE PENNINE WAY
-EDALE TO KIRK YETHOLM-

The Reluctant Hiker

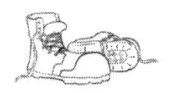

It took me a long time to decide that I was going to walk the Pennine Way. The idea of a 250 mile route following the backbone of England appealed to me well enough - I just couldn't get my head around the idea that over 10,000 people walk on it every year. I had images of an endless crocodile of people from one end to the other, of a path like a super highway eroded deep into the top of the hills, of double booked B&B's, of crowded hostels and pubs where hikers outnumbered locals. I needn't have worried - but then, it was early March and the Pennines were covered in snow.

My plane touched down in Manchester. Customs and baggage retrieval were over in a matter of minutes and I was soon on the train into the heart of the city. Manchester Piccadilly station was busy with early morning commuters. I scanned the sign boards for a train to Edale, but as I couldn't figure out which train I needed, I asked one of the attendants.

"Hang on a minute mate - I'll go an 'ave a look" he said, and disappeared into the crowd.

I assumed that was the last I would see of him, but only a couple of minutes had passed before I saw him weaving his way between the passengers to find me. He didn't just tell me where to go either - he guided me to the right platform and the right train - thanks mate!

It was a short ride to Edale. Within 40 minutes of leaving Manchester Piccadilly, I had my rucksack on my back and was heading up the road from the station to Edale village. In my hurry to get from the plane and start walking, I had forgotten to get any food or drink. There was a small shop in the village where I was able to buy the appropriate amount of junk food which forms a staple part of my hiking diet. Well, that and beer.

Kinder Scout and Bleaklow

I could see snow on Kinder Scout and the uplands of Edale Moor. The sun was shining warmly and I was full of that first day enthusiasm. That I hadn't slept since the night before last and had been travelling for about 30 hours didn't seem to be having any affect. My legs felt good, the pack weight was tolerable and the path leading out of Edale was reassuringly solid and empty. A few sheep were grazing quietly on the lower slopes. Beyond a gated wall separating the lower pastures from the uplands, the path became noticeably steeper. The grind up Crowden Brook had me panting so it was with some relief that I breasted the edge of the escarpment and emerged on to Edale Moor. So far, so good.

The flat top of Kinder Scout is only just over 2000 feet above sea level, but as the highest point on the southern Pennines, it attracts it's share of difficult weather. Before I left, I had looked at the local mountain rescue unit's web site and read some of the accounts of rescues, particularly those from the Kinder Downfall area, which seemed to attract the worst weather and the least suitably equipped hikers. Although some of the accounts were harrowing enough to make one think twice, I wasn't too worried, having walked across Kinder Scout and neighbouring Bleaklow a few times when I was at college in Matlock. Today though, the sun was reflecting off the snow lying in all the gullies, adding immeasurable to the beauty of the views.

It had been more than 30 years since I had set foot on the Pennine Way and lots had changed. In those days, much of the path was a boggy, black scar across the landscape, where countless thousands of feet had done their bit to erode the vegetation and expose the peat below. I had read that large sections of the path were now paved with enormous blocks of rock, sunk level with the upper surface of the moor. I wasn't sure whether I would like this. At first I found the surface unyielding and unnatural and began to think that it diminished the whole essence of walking on the uplands. Gradually though, as the miles accumulated, I started to appreciate those chunky blocks. Over time, they settle in to the surrounding moor, acquiring a patina of their own. As the centuries pass, they will become part of the cultural landscape, continuing to define a human pathway, just as Roman Roads and Neolithic tracks are still visible across Britain today. As long as they aren't eaten by the moor first. In some of the softer sections, some of the rocks had already begun to sink in to the ooze.

As I passed over Kinder Scout, a helicopter was buzzing back and forth, delivering parcels of rocks for the latest sections of the route. I didn't envy the workers their task of digging them in. It would be backbreaking work, often in foul conditions.

I had seriously underestimated how tired I was going to be at the end of that first day. By the time I'd struggled over Kinder Low, past Kinder Downfall and across the empty moor to Snake Pass, I was pretty much exhausted. It was already early evening; there was no way I could make it across Bleaklow to Crowden youth hostel before dark, especially since there was plenty of wet, punky snow lying around, slowing me down. Fortuitously there was a car stopped where the path hits the road so I asked them if I could get a ride to the pub just down the hill. They looked a bit surprised to be asked, but with my almost foreign accent, I think they considered me harmless enough. Inevitably, the pub was closed, so they took me to the nearest - the 'Yorkshire Bridge' a few miles further on near Ladybower reservoir. A couple of pints in the bar, a shower, then bed. I was out for the count.

I didn't bother with breakfast the next morning. I was eager to get going. I walked down the road away from the pub, stuck out my thumb, and in no time at all, was heading back up to Snake Pass with a chap I'll call Fred, early morning commuter and sometime climber. There must be something about a big rucksack full of camping gear that says 'safe enough' to motorists, as I'd had no trouble getting a ride.

Fred dropped me off at the spot where the Pennine Way crosses the road. We said our goodbyes and as he headed towards Manchester, I headed north towards Bleaklow. The snowy path was well trodden, but even so, I found my boots sinking, especially where the snow had accumulated in the hollows. I'm used to snow that squeaks under foot - this stuff squelched and had the consistency of rice. My boots and feet were soaked in minutes and before long the clouds had descended and I was walking in freezing fog. The few visible stalks of vegetation were soon covered in a thick rime.

Although much of the route had been slabbed, it was surprisingly hard to keep to the path. All the hollows had drifted in. I lost count of the times I was walking along on what seemed to be a firm crust of snow, only to crash through, sometimes up to my waist, into running water below.

Eventually, I passed the Wain Stones near Bleaklow Head and started the descent off the moor down Torside Clough to Torside Reservoir. The descent was a welcome relief as almost as soon as I started heading downwards, the sun came out and the snow disappeared. I tarried briefly at the Crowden youth hostel. It seemed to be closed, but the benches outside weren't, so I took the opportunity to do a quick sock change and grab a mouthful of something or other. There is nothing more therapeutic than a quick airing of the feet followed by a change of socks, especially if you've been sloshing about in your boots for a few miles and your feet look like prunes.

Strange Meeting on Black Hill

It's a steady slog north from Crowden, up to Laddow Rocks and on to Black Hill. So far, I had seen almost no-one since leaving Edale, but as I struggled up the path I came across another hiker taking a break and looking out over the valley. My lungs were about at bursting point from hauling my pack and my not inconsiderable bulk up the slope, so I took the opportunity to recover and share a few words. Oscar (I don't really know his name, but that's as good as any) told me that he lived in Oldham and was new to hiking. For years he had seen others heading off to the hills and thought they were daft. Why would anyone waste all that energy, only to get wet and muddy, he'd thought. Then, for some reason he didn't share, he had started walking on the Pennines himself and had become completely hooked. Now he couldn't get enough of it. He spend all his free time exploring the hills near his home. I think he was a bit surprised to hear that I had travelled over 3000 miles to walk on his hills and was even more surprised to hear that I intended to walk across all of them - well, at least all the ones in the way between Edale and Scotland. I could feel him taking that in. I don't think he'd ever considered multi-day, long distance hikes before. I like to think the idea stuck.

The Pennine Way follows the valley of Crowden Great Brook until it is nothing more than a dribble down the flank of Black Hill. As with Bleaklow, the summit of Black Hill was covered in wet snow and it had started to get chilly again. There were a few people about on the hill, one of whom used my camera to snap a picture of me standing against the trig point looking heroic. Well, I think I look heroic. That picture fascinates me. In the far distance, a hiker is visible making his way towards the summit. It's John - only I didn't know it at the time, and certainly had no idea how things would play out over the next few days.

John walked up as I retrieved my camera and pulled my gear together. I can't exactly remember how the conversation went. He probably asked me where I was heading, detecting from my accent that I wasn't a local, and from my monstrous backpack, that I wasn't just out

Actually, I'm English

for the day. I was starting to get a bit chilled and was eager to get going, and was a bit surprised to hear him ask if I minded a bit of company for a while. What could I say? "I'm an anti-social sod who came over here to be alone"? No, that would sound a bit rude, and anyway, just at that moment, I didn't really mind the idea of some company for a mile or two.

John looked as though he might be a fit, capable walker. He was certainly dressed for business, with proper boots and gaiters, a thick polar fleece jacket and a small day pack - good gear, that looked as though it had seen a mile or two. I guessed that we were about the same age but whereas my hair seems to have slipped from my head to my face, John sported a full crop of steel grey hair and was clean shaven. I towered over him, but as I soon found out, size isn't everything.

We set off north along the Pennine Way, heading for the crossing of A635 at Wessenden Head. I think I must have misheard him. I thought he'd mentioned something about a car at the road and a trip to a pub, so I was mightily surprised when he just carried on across the road, heading down a track along side a series of reservoirs at a blistering pace. It was only about 4 miles from where we had met on Black Hill to Marsden, but since this was only my second day, my legs were beginning to feel it and I was getting tired. I think John realised that I wasn't good for many more miles and anyway, my appetite for a pint had been awakened. The New Inn offered beer, food and a bed - good enough for me! As we sat chatting over pints, John asked me if I would be continuing along the Pennine Way in the morning.

"Here, take this beer mat. You have to cross the M62 on the foot bridge. Just drop it in the middle of the path. If I'm up that way and there's no beer mat, I'll know you haven't got there yet - if there is, I'll know I've missed you."

He drained his pint and headed out of the door, leaving me to settle in to my room, assuming it would be the last I would see of him.

The morning came far too soon, but fortified by a massive breakfast, composed mainly of meat products, I was soon fit to move again. By diverting to Marsden, we had actually abandoned the Pennine Way for a while but I was able to take a short cut over Close Moss to rejoin the main route at White Hill. Hill is a bit of a misnomer for this chunk of moor - it's really just another flattish spot, distinguished only by its white painted trig point. I stopped, slumped my rucksack against it and took the obligatory picture. I have countless pictures of my rucksack leaning against trig points, each one as pointless and uninformative as the next.

From White Hill, the path leads gradually down towards the A672. Long before I got to the road, I could see John walking the last few steps back from the north. He'd obviously been down to the motorway bridge, cruising for beer mats and was making his was back to the tea stand at the road. The morning had been going well and I was entirely happy plugging along on my own, but I found myself rather pleased to see him. We had not even come close to exhausting mutually interesting topics of conversation the night before - indeed, we had only just begun to explore the many things we had in common. Another day hiking with John? No problem at all.

What I hadn't realised is that when John left me in Marsden, he'd had to walk at least 7 miles back to his home, then back-track the same distance the following morning to meet me at the bridge. As I subsequently learned, he used to be a competitive fell runner and was still a keen competitor at the local level. A few miles here or there didn't seem to bother him at all - in fact, he relished them.

My third day rolled swiftly by in a blur of conversation. We stopped for a scenic breather on Blackstone Edge and had a bit of a chuckle as both of us immediately took our boots and socks off to give our feet a breather, even though there was snow in the hollows and it was fairly cool.

I managed to talk John in to an early lunchtime pint at The White House pub where the path crosses the road between Ripponden and Littleborough. The beer was acceptable, but I don't think either of us were greatly impressed with the atmosphere. It seemed to favour a business clientèle, not sweaty, out-of-season hikers.

My body still hadn't completely accepted that hiking all day was going to be its daily punishment, and it told me so through tired legs and shortness of breath on the inclines. I like to think it was because I was carrying 35lbs of camping gear, clothes and camera stuff but the reality was, I just wasn't fit enough yet. Certainly I wasn't fit enough to keep up with the Energizer Bunny who, with far less personal mass to carry and only a day pack, glided along tirelessly while I panted and called for breaks.

We had another break at the Stoodley Pike Monument - a honking great, dark stone pillar, originally built to commemorate the defeat of Napoleon. As we stood on the balcony, looking out over Todmorden and the valley of the River Calder, John asked me what my plans were for the night. So far, I'd been a bit of a wimp, staying in pubs the first two nights. It was time to make friends with the outdoors again.

"I think I'll find a quiet spot somewhere and hang up my hammock".

He knew of a small belt of woods just above Hebden Bridge that might be suitable, so we aimed for there. During our walk we had discussed our various strategies for camping and John was eager to see the hammock in action. I should point out that this isn't just any old hammock that you might hang from your laundry pole and the fence in your back garden. My Clark Jungle Hammock is a high quality, fully four season hanging tent, complete with a waterproof rain fly, enclosed sleeping area and a full fly screen, made to the same high standards as the best mountaineering equipment. It takes a while to get used to, but once you've got the hang of sleeping in it, it's really comfortable.

As we entered the woods I looked for a couple of smallish trees about 10 feet apart. In Canada, that's never a problem. On the UK's bare moors and mountains that's more of an issue, although in a pinch, I can pitch it as a rather weird one person tent. I think John was rather surprised that the trees I chose were half way up a steep slope, but once the hammock is hanging, what's below is irrelevant.

The sun was going down fast, the light was beginning to fade and John was still about 9 miles from home, so we said our goodbyes and he walked off through the woods. I had really enjoyed our time together. We shared the same humour and we both liked to spice our outdoor pursuits with a bit of discomfort and danger. There's nothing like sharing 'war' stories with someone who can visualize the conditions and has been in similar situations themselves. Sadly, I doubted that I would ever see him again.

Five minutes later, John reappeared. He had been hoping to walk east along the south side of the Rochdale Canal but had found his way blocked. He had no alternative but to retrace his steps, say goodbye to me all over again, and head down to the canal, cross at the locks and make his way home through Hebden Bridge. I like to think he caught a bus or train - I'll bet he walked!

Stranger in a Strange Land

That night it froze hard. I awoke to a thick rime of frost on the inside of the hammock and the top of the fly sheet was white. I was toasty in my sleeping bag but my bladder was full. Over the years I have perfected a method of peeing without getting out of the hammock. It involves lots of zippers, some gymnastics and a fair bit of balance. Oh yes - and remembering not to leave the boots and rucksack directly below........., but this wasn't the time for gymnastics, it was time to get going. I quickly undid the hammock, took care of the most pressing business, dressed, shook the ice off the flysheet, stuffed everything in my rucksack and headed down the hill, over the canal, past the hippy village and on towards Hebden Bridge.

Almost immediately, my nostrils were assaulted by the smell of cooking bacon, coming from a roadside sandwich van. While the owner poured me a coffee and cooked my breakfast, he asked me which part of the States I was from and seemed vaguely disappointed to hear that I was only a former Brit living in Canada. I listened politely while he told me about his travels in the US. Fortunately my breakfast was soon ready and I was able to escape to a nearby bench to eat in peace. I needed some space; the breakfast bacon, egg, sausage breakfast bun was enormous. I thought is was supposed to be North Americans who ate massive meals - clearly I still had a lot to learn about the 'new' Britain.

The road up through Heptonstall had me stopping and panting every few yards. People who live around there, if they walk at all, must be really fit. Fortunately it was a short, sharp climb which began to level out as I rejoined the Pennine Way across Heptonstall Moor. It's rare to get a real, visual sense of progress, but I looked back across the valley and there stood Stoodley Pike prominently on the valley edge. Only a few hours had passed since John and I were standing there together but it looked many miles away.

The path across Heptonstall Moor was damp and boggy - a well used rut across the landscape - but it was mercifully empty of other people so once again, I was able to enjoy the company of skylarks and curlews.

It wasn't long before the Pennine Way joined briefly with the Pennine Bridleway - a broader track open to horses and bicycles. At the gate above one of the Gorple Reservoirs, I stopped briefly for a rest. I could see a cyclist labouring up the slope from the dam, so I opened the gate so he didn't have to break stride or dismount, receiving a perfunctory nod of gratitude in return.

The next few miles were a long slog uphill past the Walshaw Dean

Reservoirs towards Withins Height. The building remains near the top of the hill at 'Top Withins' don't look particularly ancient. While their origins were in the 16th century, the farm complex was still standing and occupied in the 1920s. The isolated location and dark walls are are reputed to have been the inspiration for Heathcliffe's 'Wuthering Heights' in Emily Bronte's novel. This tenuous connection is enough to draw people from all over the world to see the rather unimpressive ruins. Some of the signage in the area is in both English and Japanese.

I didn't tarry at the ruins but plugged on by. A notation on my map suggested that there were two pubs in Stanbury - a mere 1 ½ miles down the valley. There were a few people on this part of the path but I had no time for social discourse other than a quick 'hello'. Suddenly my legs were tireless, my pack felt lighter and the ground started to fly underneath my feet. I could already taste the first pint. I made Stanbury just after 12.

Stanbury is a single street village, with modest stone houses crowding the road, leaving barely enough space for a walker - especially one carrying a heavy rucksack - between their flat fronts and the narrow road. I arrived, sweaty and thirsty at the first pub I found. It was called "The Friendly", but struggled to live up to its ambitious name. I was treated with practised disinterest by the landlady, who served me as if I was a mild annoyance. I suppose I can't blame her. In the summer she must have to cater to an endless stream of foreign sounding tourists, all of whom expect quaint 'olde English' hospitality. My North American accent and my rucksack must have thrown me firmly in that camp. I hadn't expected to be treated as a local or a long-lost cousin, but some basic warmth and civility would have been welcome. Not surprisingly, I only stayed long enough to gulp down a couple of pints and a bag of crisps and headed out the door looking for a less chilly spot to spend my lunchtime.

Within a couple of hundred yards I came across the Old Silent Inn, a formidable barn of a pub, one wall of which rose vertically from the edge of the road. From the outside, I formed the impression that it may have been recently 'done' to attract people more interested in old beams, warm fire-places and fine pub food than in a greasy bar and copious booze. I wasn't wrong. Nevertheless, I was greeted with a modest welcome and somewhat to my surprise, wasn't made to feel out of place when I settled myself and my gear near the big log fire to consume the pint of John Smith's I'd just ordered. Another soon followed. Still, my enthusiasm for lunchtime pints was definitely on the wane. After a few minutes I drained the rest of my pint, shouldered my pack and headed somewhat groggily into the sunlight.

Although it was only another three miles to Cowling, it felt far more. Whether it was the lunchtime beer or the soggy footing, the long grind up to the top of Ickornshaw Moor seemed interminable. I was glad when I was on the downhill side and had already started to think about a long, hot shower and a comfortable bed.

There's not much to Cowling and I was beginning to wonder whether I would have to forego the shower and bed and spend another night on the moor, but as I headed towards the biggest cluster of houses I saw an elderly lady hobbling along towards me. Yes, there was a B&B up one of the side streets. I proceeded. I knocked. I was shown to my room with a comfortable bed and shower. I washed. I slept. I accidentally left them a pair of my best socks, freshly washed, on the radiator.

Onward to Malham

I wasn't the only hiker in the B&B that night. A middle aged couple from somewhere in the Midlands, by their accents anyway, were also out and about on the Pennine Way. They were doing the route in small chunks; a couple of days here and there as they could find the time and the energy. Although getting out in the hills is always good for the soul and I admired them for that, stringing together completion of the route over a long time seemed a bit pointless to me. I needed to do it in one meaty chunk - or not at all. I would have no sense of achievement if it had all been bits and pieces. Of course, I didn't tell them that. After breakfast we went our separate ways.

Between Cowling and Gargrave, the Pennine Way crosses a landscape of low, rounded hills, stone walls and sheep pasture, criss-crossed by innumerable small roads which link a multitude of farms to the nearby villages of Earby, Cononley, Carleton-in-Craven and many others. Although the hills were empty of other hikers, the land felt occupied, owned and managed - quite different to the open moors. I know the moors are equally managed and maintained, but I savour the illusion of the wild. The highest point on this leg was the beacon at Pinhaw (388m.) - a mere pimple, and surrounded by the only bit of moorland I was to see that day.

The couple from the B&B were sitting eating a sandwich at Thornton-in-Craven as I passed by. I had seen them heading for the village from a couple of fields away. They had managed to follow the proper course of the Pennine Way, across the Roman Road and into the village. I had somehow ended up well to the south of where I should have been and had added a about half a mile to my trip. I think they must have seen me too, if the slightly smug expressions on their faces were anything to go by. They were probably thinking something uncharitable about daft foreigners not being able to read a map.

A short hop from Thornton-in-Craven brought me to the banks of the Leeds and Liverpool Canal and a brief, relaxing stroll along the canal tow-path. East Marton church sits all on its own in a field on the other side of the canal but out of reach for this lazy hiker who had no intentions of back-tracking. A canal longboat was tied up, just before the bridge to the village, but there were no signs of life on board and there was nobody around so I didn't linger. Gargrave was only a couple of miles ahead and as it was well past lunchtime, my inner glutton was looking forward to a pint of something cool and refreshing, preferably to wash down something pastry covered and greasy. As I entered the village, almost the first thing to catch my eye was the 'Mason's Arms' sign on the low, stone building diagonally opposite the church – conveniently located for a Sunday pint after Mattins. This wasn't Sunday, but the pub was open, I was thirsty and I had some pound coins eating a hole in my fanny-pack. Despite its low, beamed ceilings and cheery fireplace, the pub was a bit of a disappointment. All the elements were there, but somehow it lacked character, so I quickly downed my pint and headed further into the village to look for some food.

I availed myself of the excellent selection of plastic-wrapped sausage rolls and cartons of strawberry milk available at the Co-op, on the narrow High Street, and settled down on the bench outside to watch the traffic. It was fine entertainment to see large commercial vehicles thread their way through the village, narrowly missing cars parked with two wheels on the road and two on the pavement. The drivers skill and sense of distance was amazing - they would swing their vehicles around with apparent ease.

Leaving Gargrave, the Pennine Way crosses the canal at a low bridge, just down from a lock. An elderly local seemed a bit surprised that I would want to take a picture of something as humdrum as a canal lock, so I played the American tourist for a while and assured him that it was my duty to take pictures of everything for 'the folks back home'.

I walked on. A short rise over Eshton Moor through stone wall enclosed, sheep filled pastures led back down to the valley of the Aire. The sheep had close-cropped the grass, but the route of the Pennine Way was clearly visible as a linear stain where countless feet had bruised the grass and compacted the ground below. For the next four miles, the path closely followed the river. It looked simple enough on the map, but predictably, I managed to get diverted and ended up fighting through thick vegetation, over barbed wire topped walls and boggy ground until I regained the route near Hanlith. The steep climb past Hanlith Hall in a thunderstorm nearly exhausted my few remaining shreds of energy, but there was a pay-off. As the clouds moved off, a wonderful rainbow spanned the valley.

I hadn't made any plans for accommodation and had vaguely been thinking of bivvying somewhere above Malham Cove. In the end though, as I walked through the village, the thought of a few pints at the Lister Arms and a cheap bed in the warmth and comfort of the nearby Youth Hostel won me over. Unusually, I chose quality over quantity. After a delicious pint of Thwaites Lancaster Bomber – a new one on me – I returned to the hostel, sent a few messages to loved ones back in Canada, and turned in early.

On Pen-Y-Ghent with Mr. Sociable

In the morning a thick rime of frost covered the landscape and the Rooks were making a celebratory racket as I ambled through the village heading for Malham Cove. The frost accentuated the lynchets – those remnants of medieval agriculture – making them stand out prominently in the fields.

Malham Cove is undeniably lovely. The high limestone cliffs tower over the valley, the stream unexpectedly bubbling from its base to join with Gordale Beck to become the Aire River. At most times of the year, the area is crawling with visitors, but at 7am in early March, I had the place to myself, although I didn't tarry long. It was only about 13 miles to Horton-in-Ribblesdale, but they promised to be a fairly tough ones and I wanted to get moving.

I clambered up the path to the limestone pavement above the cove, made yet more famous as a camping spot during the hunt for the Deathly Hallows in the Harry Potter movies, then started up the dry valley where the river used to run before being swallowed by the rocks. The air was still and very peaceful; the sound of my foot steps echoing from the cliffs being virtually the only sound. As the frost melted, a thick mist accumulated and only partially cleared as I circumnavigated Malham Tarn.

Just about anyone who has grown up in Britain or has the slightest interest in geography has heard of Malham Tarn. It's the highest lake in England and the highest marl lake in the UK, yet really, with a surface area of 62 hectares it's little more than a pond. At least, that is how it appears to someone from the Canadian Shield country of Canada, where something that small would barely rate a name. But, we're not in Canada, are we – and Malham Tarn was quite beautiful with the mist rising gently as the sun started to emerge.

Other than the high country around Kinder Scout and Bleaklow at the start of the Pennine Way, much of the first 80 miles of the route had been across sheep pasture, through farms, and across low limestone hills; more pastoral than wild. This gradually began to change beyond Malham with the steady climb up to the summit of Fountains Fell. At 2,192 feet, it was the highest elevation I had reached so far, although it's flattish top, pitted with old coal mining and lead smelting works, barely rates as the most impressive peak. There was plenty of snow in the gullies and piled up on the lee side of walls. It didn't take much to recognise that despite its rounded form, Fountains Fell could attract some brutal weather.

Despite the heavy grey clouds, the air was still and clear, so I had an excellent view west to Pen-y-Ghent and the lower hills beyond. Pen-y-Ghent is a giant whale-back of a hill. Beyond it is the village of Horton-in-Ribblesdale where I intended to stay. The previous night, while at Malham YHA, I had been in electronic contact with my niece Madeleine and her husband who were heading south from a few days on Hadrian's Wall. The plan was to meet up in a pub in Horton for Sunday lunch, which meant that I would have a a few hours of relaxation in the morning and no need for an early start. As it turned out, that was a very good thing.

The path up Pen-y-Ghent looks a bit intimidating from the bottom as it seems to get steeper and steeper until the final few yards are a scramble up an almost vertical face. At least – that's how it looks from the bottom. By this point in the day, my pack had started to feel a bit heavy. While I was taking a breather before the climb, I met two young chaps from London who were out for a weekend of adventure. I can't remember their names so let's call them Bert and Ernie. I had been fully intending to stay at one of the pubs, but as we chatted, they told me of a camp site they were using, which was much cheaper. As it was the weekend the pubs were probably booked up anyway, so I determined to look into it.

In the end, the climb up Pen-y-Ghent was less of a struggle than I had been expecting. Despite my pack, I even managed to overtake a few day-hikers. After a week of steady hiking, my legs and lungs had adjusted, so although I was tired at the end of each day, I was starting to feel fit and energetic.

The summit was crowded! There must have been twenty or more people hanging around, taking pictures, squatting on rocks, eating sandwiches and generally relaxing. Most of the clouds I had seen from Fountains Fell had dissipated and the views were extensive and grand. I couldn't wait to get off there.

The path down to Horton-in-Ribblesdale was awash with hikers. The occasional person looked as though they might know what they were doing, but most were ill equipped, out of condition and struggling laboriously up the long grind to the summit. That much of the path was across deep snow did nothing to help their progress as they trudged up the narrow groove which countless feet had worn. I have to admit, I lost patience and instead of waiting my turn to negotiate some of the more tricky sections, I ignored the path altogether and stomped off through the untrammelled snow field, sinking knee deep, but keeping balance with my hiking sticks. I heard a few irate 'well's and other expressions of disgust at my impatience – but frankly Scarlett..................

Down in the village I found the camp site that Bert and Ernie had mentioned. It was just a small field attached to a farm, with rudimentary toilet and washing facilities. It seemed fine to me. There were even a couple of small trees from which to sling my hammock. I had barely finished setting up my accommodation and sorting out my bedding when Bert and Ernie returned. After a quick look at my hammock, which they declared 'unusual, but interesting' we headed for the Golden Lion.

When I say it was a long evening, I'm not suggesting that the time wore heavily on our hands. We started off in the late afternoon, and while I can't quite remember how or why we left, I have no doubt that closing time may have had something to do with it. Beer flowed freely. Whenever there was an empty glass on the table, someone would jump up to fill it or buy another round. I know we talked about hiking adventures, and I undoubtedly bored them with tales of Canadian wilderness canoe trips, bear safety, leeches, blackflies and all my other favourite topics as soon as I have a captive audience. I have a dim recollection that there was an important soccer match on the big screen TV in the corner but I have no idea who was playing whom, or why. No doubt we staggered back to the camp site in the dark but that part of my memory is blank.

Morning inevitably came, and along with it a certain fuzziness. Even before I disentangled myself from my hammock, through the fly-screen I could see (and hear) Bert retching. He'd only just made it out of the tent. As you can imagine, as they packed their car for the next leg of their adventure and I disassembled my camp, we all felt as though we were wading through molasses.

I had a few hours to kill. My first stop was the Pen-y-ghent Café just along the street where some baked beans on toast and a big mug of coffee went some way to settling my internal disturbances. I also bought a pair of my favourite Ultramax socks to replace the ones I'd left in Cowling. After that, the time dragged until lunchtime. I made my way over to the Crown, where I was scheduled to meet Maddy and John, but the pub wasn't opening until just before lunchtime. In the end, I just walked a short distance up the farm track to the rear of the pub – the route of the Pennine Way – sat on my rucksack and waited.

Mercifully, Maddy and John arrived on time, the pub opened and we went inside for beer and lunch. For me, it really was the hair of the dog, especially since a big, brindled, magnificently ugly mastiff was lying under the adjacent table. Truly, he was one of the most homely dogs I have ever met, but like almost all dogs in English pubs, was quiet and well behaved, even when other dogs came into the room. I swear all English dogs have been lobotomised. There is so little 'dog' left in them.

Maddy, John and I had an excellent lunch and an excellent chat, then they resumed their journey south towards Birmingham and I headed north up the Pennine Way towards Hawes. It's about 12 miles from Horton-in-Ribblesdale to Hawes, almost all of it along stone wall-lined tracks. After the excesses of the night before and the long wait, I had been eager to get going, but time wasn't on my side. Daylight was beginning to fade by the time I got to the nature reserve at Ling Gill – a deep limestone gorge retaining natural flora and fauna – and I briefly considered camping on the level ground next to the stream. But I hadn't walked enough that day. Despite the booze, or perhaps because of it, I was full of unspent energy and needed to wear off some of those extra calories.

It's a good job that section of the Pennine Way follows old but well defined tracks because the surrounding limestone hills are riddled with pot holes and caves and the light was going fast. With my propensity for following sheep paths, I could have easily have found myself in trouble had the route not been as well defined as it was, although while the light was still good, I had a great view west to the long, high ridge of Whernside – one of the 'three peaks' (along with Ingleborough and Pen-y-Ghent) of fell running fame.

Eventually it became so dark that I resorted to using my headlamp. I hadn't ever needed to use one before and wasn't quite sure what to expect, but soon found that I really enjoyed stumbling along in its pool of light – and I mean stumbling. The track was paved with rounded rocks of varying sizes, all conveniently arranged so that anything resembling a normal gait was impossible. At first I kept looking for a suitable place to pitch my hammock, or even for a spot of flattish ground where I could pitch it as a bivvy, but none presented themselves. All I could see was steep slopes, stone walls and the narrow cobbled path. I walked on.

Instead of following the last couple of miles across Ten End to Hawes, I carried on along the track until it blended with a slightly larger one leading towards the village. I decided it was too late and I was too tired to be bothered trying to find accommodation in the village, so I pitched my bivvy on the narrow grass verge at the side of the road, pegged everything as well as I could against the increasingly vigorous wind, and promptly fell asleep.

Hawes, Keld and Middleton-in-Teesdale

Hawes was bathed in sunlight as I approached in the morning. Most of the shops were still closed but I managed to find one that sold me a box of milk, some cheese and bread, which I hastily demolished while sitting on a bench outside the Hawes Club (Snooker and Games – Casual Membership Available). I like Hawes. It seems an honest little town, almost exclusively comprised of stone buildings, many of them old industrial mills and factories along the Gayle Beck. I imagine that it would be chock full of tourists in the summer, but at 7.30am on a Monday morning, other than a few delivery vehicles, the streets were empty.

By about 8.15, my stomach was full, I had food and water in my pack and I was ready for the next section to Keld. In my mind, Keld was about the half-way point. In reality, somewhat more of the Pennine Way lies to the north of Keld than to the south, but it is also the place where Wainwright's 'Coast to Coast' path crosses, neatly dividing it into two halves.

By this point in the hike I had really hit my stride. Through careful foot management, frequent airings and sock changes and good boots, my feet were completely free of any abrasions or hot spots and they no longer felt any more tired than the rest of me by the end of the day. I had come to terms with my pack. It still felt good to be able to put it down from time to time, but carrying it was no longer the Herculean task it had seemed at Edale. While the long, unremitting climb up to Great Shunner Fell was arduous, it didn't seem interminable. Well, most of it didn't! Somewhere along that section I must have followed a sheep path which ended in a boggy mess of peat hags, dead ends, green slimy pools and knee deep heather. I had no choice but to struggle through following a compass bearing until I regained the path. That dissolved some of my energy, and a bit of my confidence with it. There was still plenty of snow around on the hill tops and I rested briefly from the biting wind in one of the stone hunter's blinds which dot the landscape. Unfortunately, it didn't provide much shelter, so I was soon moving again.

If anything, the grind down from Great Shunner Fell seemed just as difficult as the grind up. Even though my body was feeling good, my mind was over-active. I was doing that thing hikers should never do: I was thinking ahead, wishing I was already at Keld, instead of enjoying each moment as it unfolded. I tried to re-engage, but having sent my mind on ahead, it was now searching for a cosy pub to slake my thirst and rest my body. It found one too – the Kearton Hotel Bar in Thwaite. My body soon caught up.

One pint for thirst, one for taste then I was back on the road again. From Thwaite the Pennine Way takes a rather gratuitous loop around Kisdon Hill to reach Keld. I chose to amble a more direct route through Angram. Mercifully, the old Youth Hostel – now the Keld Lodge – was open for business. There were few people in the Lodge that night so, after a decent curry I ended up chatting to the owner for quite a while until I headed for bed.

Leaving Keld, I immediately took the wrong path and ended up heading south along the stretch of path I'd avoided the previous day. This was fortuitousness as it gave me an opportunity to see the lovely waterfall just east of the village. The rest of the morning was an easy walk up the east side of Stonesdale Beck Valley, past old stone barns and the old coal mine workings near Tan Hill. Tan Hill pub is the last remaining building of a once extensive settlement. It now stands alone, spare and unsheltered on the moor with no other building visible for miles in all directions. I couldn't pass up the opportunity for some liquid refreshment and ordered a pint from the frazzled owner who immediately offered to sell me the place. I must say, it was a bit tempting. The only neighbours I could see were two very young lambs who couldn't quite decide whether they should be inside or outside, their horny little feet skittering on the hard stone floors.

I had a chat with one of the bar-tenders who had walked the Pennine Way himself a few years before. He strongly advised me not to follow the path across Sleightholme Moor but to stick to the road and then a farm track towards Sleightholme Farm, in order to avoid a very boggy section. I don't think I missed much by taking his advise.

The days pass, my mind is constantly busy, yet if you asked me what I think about when I'm walking, I wouldn't be able to tell you. The amount of mental effort necessary to keep putting one foot in front of the other is minimal, yet my brain churns away, doing whatever it's doing with no conscious input. I don't get lonely. I don't long for the company of others. I'm usually happy to stop and chat with anyone I meet, but there was no-one on my section of the Pennine Way this day, and that was fine by me.

Shortly after crossing God's Bridge – a natural stone arch over the

River Greta - I hit the A66 dual carriageway. Someone had the forethought to provide a tunnel so that hikers didn't end up joining the badgers and rabbits mashed to pulp on the road.

I have little memory of the long moorland section between the A66 and the reservoirs in the valley of the River Balder. My photographs show that it was sunny and warm, with a well trodden path leading straight across flattish moorland. Perhaps I was lost in thought. Perhaps I was so enraptured by the song of the skylarks, that I didn't notice the passing of the miles. Perhaps there was nothing outstanding about that section to make it memorable.

By the time I crossed the end of Blackton Reservoir my legs were beginning to feel the day, even though I had only walked about 12 miles from Keld. Some days are like that. Sometimes the miles skip effortlessly by; others, every yard is hard fought. This day was somewhere in the middle. I still had a few miles to go before Middleton-in-Teesdale, and a night under the stars wasn't really an option. Foolishly I'd failed to provision myself adequately. All my consumables were consumed and all my liquid was gone. Whether I liked it or not, I was going to make Middleton-in-Teesdale or face a hungry and thirsty night. It's amazing how a little need can focus the mind. Those last few miles zipped by. I arrived in the village just in time to buy some food and drink and look around for somewhere to stay.

The options were limited so I knocked on the door of the first B&B I came to. After getting a suspicious eye-balling from the landlady, who, quite reasonably, must have wondered what kind of foreign nut would be passing through in March, I was admitted to an inner sanctum of doilies and collector plates. My room was blessedly free of most of these things and after a quick shower and change of clothes, I headed back along the High Street to find something to eat. It's likely that I ate some fish and chips on a bench, but like the moors earlier in the day, if I did, they just weren't that memorable.

An Unexpected Encounter

I had been looking forward to the next day for a while. My map showed me that the first half was a path along the Tees River, with gentle gradients, waterfalls and some crags. After that, the geomorphological wonder of High Cup Nick and a descent into the village of Dufton. A nice lazy morning with no climbs, good footing and pleasant scenery suited me fine. The second half of the day, including where I was going to stay that night would unfold eventually. For now though, the first few miles of trail lay right along the river – in places, a narrow path with a high stone wall on one side and steep, eroding river bank on the other. As usual, no one else was about and it didn't take me long to find my rhythm, let the lizard brain control the walking and set my conscious mind loose to go wherever it goes.

My conscious mind was about to get a big shock. It had to come scuttling back from wherever it had been because there on the path ahead and coming my way quickly, was another hiker. Rucksack, gaiters, fleece jacket, steel grey hair – good God, it was John!

At first I thought, what a coincidence that we should end up walking on the same section of path. Then it dawned on me that he had worked out where I might be and set out to see if he could intercept me. If I were a more timid or suspicious person I might have begun to wonder whether I was being stalked. Fortunately I'm not and I was just pleased to see him, although completely shocked that he had been able to figure out where I would be and had bothered to try.

We sat down and assessed our options. After spending the night camped above Cauldron Snout, John had set off towards Middleton-in-Teesdale heading for some breakfast. I wasn't too eager to retrace my steps, and he didn't really seem to mind retracing his, so we had a quick review of our supplies and decided that we had enough to last as far as Dufton, our destination for the end of the day. I offered John a chunk of Wensleydale I had in my top pack. I'm not sure whether it was the crumbs, the dog hair - how that stuff gets everywhere, I'll never know - or his lactose intolerance that made him decide he wasn't interested. He had a few health-food bars; I had a few biscuits and half a Mars Bar. Good enough.

The path along the Tees was impossibly scenic. A thin mist hung over the river, soaking the moss covered trees which clung to the steep banks. The water raced along, roaring over the waterfalls at Low Force and High Force with impressive.....well, force. Once again, there was no one else around and we were able to enjoy the scenery mercifully free of the crowds of gawkers which seem to plague every attractive place in the UK. Perhaps the falls were too far from the nearest car park to be much of a tourist attraction. At a bridge across Harwood Beck we passed my favourite road sign ever: "WARNING. Anyone caught exceeding 5mph will be stoned to death – THIS MEANS YOU".

The path climbed steadily, closely following the river, turning away from the inhabited valley and back in to the moors. A thick mist descended, obscuring all but the lower few feet of the crags and talus slopes at Falcon Clints. Mist does strange things with sound, blocking out some, accentuating others. The cawing of crows pierced the mist, but most other sounds, including our footfalls were oddly muffled. We found ourselves speaking in lowered voices, as if we were listening for something. Perhaps people retain some fragment of the wariness of our ancestors, from a time when Cave Bears and Dire Wolves roamed the wilds.

We stopped briefly for me to take a picture of Cauldron Snout, where the Tees cascades down the rocks below Cow Green Reservoir, then plugged along in the mist towards High Cup Nick. I had been looking forward to seeing this impressive void, where glaciers gouged a deep divot out of the surrounding limestone, exposing the harder, igneous rocks of the Whin Sill, for as long as I can remember. Geomorphology was just about the only thing I paid attention to in grammar school and features like Malham Cove and High Cup Nick had figured prominently in my developing view of the world around me.

As usual, John set a blistering pace which had me grunting and sweating beneath my pack while he barely seemed to touch the ground. We could sense High Cup Nick as a giant void in the earth, long before we reached its edge. The mist was so thick, there was no chance of seeing anything. We could hear the crows calling in the mist, but from its edge, there was no way to gauge the extent of the chasm. There was nothing to photograph, nothing to do, actually, but keep on walking. I promised myself that one day I would come back when the air was clear. It's a promise I have yet to keep.

It was damp and cool during the rest of the descent to Dufton. I have a picture of John, leaning against a stone wall, looking out over the valley to the village below. The mist is still hanging around on the higher ground, but the valley is clear and is lit with that late afternoon light that shines beneath the clouds. He looks as fresh as a daisy – darn him. After almost 20 miles, I was feeling anything but fresh and was in serious need of some liquid refreshment.

Dufton is built around a broad, long village green with stone houses set well back from the main road. I immediately like it. It felt calm and quiet – perhaps a little too quiet. There were few cars and no traffic. A lone boy was riding his red bicycle. When he saw us, he circled around, as if he wasn't quite sure what to make of us strangers.

Inside the Stag, a cheery fire was burning in the fireplace and beer was on tap. We loosened our boots, removed a few outer layers and settled in. Before long the warmth from the fire and the alcohol had removed any residual chill. We drank. We ate, but before we got too muddy headed, our thoughts turned to finding somewhere to stay for the night. John was all for waiting until it was dark then throwing our shelters up on the village green. In retrospect, it was a great idea, but at the time I lobbied strongly for finding a B&B. Other folks in the pub provided some suggestions about accommodation, finally agreeing that a B&B at the far end of the village would probably take us in even if they weren't officially open yet. Before we knew it, the bar-tender was on the phone, arrangements were made, and we were making our way there. The B&B was in a large sandstone house. Our host was waiting for us when we arrived, showed us to our room and left us to settle in.

Cold on Cross Fell

I was the first to leave in the morning. John was heading back home by train from nearby Appleby-in-Westmorland; I was heading up the long haul to Alston via Knock Fell and Cross Fell, the latter, at 2782 feet being the highest point on the English section of the Pennine Way. As I left Dufton, John was standing in the front doorway watching my departure. Once again, I suspect we both assumed that would be the last we saw of one another. It would not be. While it was the last time I saw him on this trip, our paths would next cross a couple of years later, but that is a tale for another day.

The day was cool and blustery. For the first couple of miles, I followed a farm track over the shoulder of Dufton Pike, before steadily climbing past Brownber Hill and the wonderfully named High Scald Fell. No doubt the name has a more prosaic meaning, but I had visions of some careless hiker dousing his hand with a billy of boiling water. The lower slopes of all the hills were snow free and dull green and brown; the tops were snow covered, with deep snow filling all the gullies. I suppose I shouldn't have been surprised. It was mid-March and I had already encountered plenty of snow on Kinder Scout and Bleaklow, well to the south.

As I slowly made my way up Knock Old Man the wind started to pick up, gaining strength as I reached the paved road up to the radar station on the top of Great Dun Fell. The radar station is fenced, so rather than cross the icy slope at the front of the installation, I circumnavigated around the back, through soft, knee deep snow. It was tough going. At one point the wind caught my pack and I stumbled, leaning heavily on my hiking poles, one of which instantly folded under the weight, depositing me face first in the snow.

I rely heavily on my hiking poles. I've become pretty adept at using them, both up hill and down hill. They take some of the weight and strain off my knees and provide extra points of balance when the going gets rough. I used to think they were a bit sissy, but I long ago stopped worrying about that. The pole wasn't salvageable. From now on I would have to rely on just one to keep me out of trouble.

There's relatively little change in elevation from Great Dun Fell, over Little Dun Fell to Cross Fell, but the weather conditions were changing fast. Wind was howling up the slope from the south-west, tearing at my clothes and setting my loose pant legs flapping wildly. There was only a thin skim of crystalline snow covering the summit of Cross Fell, but the cold air and the wind drove me off quickly. Had the weather been more suitable, I would have screwed my camera on to the top of my pole, jammed the pole in the ground, set the timer, then posed by the cairn. Not this time. My boots were sopping wet from wading through the deep snow behind the radar station and I was getting seriously chilled.

I knew that 'Greg's Hut' was only a mile off the summit. At least it offered some relief from the wind and a chance to sit for a few moments. Greg's Hut is a former lead worker's cottage – now a shelter maintained by the Mountain Bothies Association – that provides a refuge for people such as myself to get out of the worst of the weather.

It's at times like this that it is easy to see why every year people die on British hills. Inadequate gear, poor preparation, lack of fitness, lousy navigation skills and an underestimation of distance and effort can turn a gentle hike in to an endurance test in no time. Add in cold, wet and wind and it can quickly become a struggle for survival. In 2010, the year I hiked the Pennine Way, 53 people died on British mountains. Admittedly, those numbers were a bit higher than the average (3 people died from lightning strikes alone), but the fact remains that they can be dangerous places.

Inside, the bothy it was stone cold! No roaring fire greeted my arrival. The thick walls broke the wind but did nothing to raise my temperature. It was bleak and sparsely furnished – just a few plastic chairs on the wet flagstone floor. Some kind person had left some bottled water and some basic food but I left them untouched for someone more needy than me. I took off my boots, wrung out my socks and put my boots back on. There was nothing I could do to dry them out, but the removal of most of the water provided some temporary relief. Within ten minutes I was back out in the wind, picking up speed along the long, winding mining track across the moor and down towards Garrigill, to raise my body temperature.

Once again, the Ordnance Survey let me down. Clearly marked on the map, right opposite the word 'Garrigill' and just near the cross indicating a church, were those two, wonderful little letters, PH, capitalized for emphasis. I had visions of walking in to a warm room, the scent of old beer hanging in the air, of placing my rucksack carefully in the corner, of taking a quick look at the treats on offer, then of asking the barman for 'a pint of Black Sheep and a packet of salt and vinegar crisps please'. I could almost taste them already.

I found the pub with no trouble; the sign said, 'George and Dragon, Free House', exactly where it was shown on the map. But instead of warmth and refreshment, I was rebuffed by boarded windows and a firmly nailed door. It's not often that I feel my spirits sinking but they did then. I had no desire to walk another 4 miles to Alston. I wasn't even sure I could.

Of course I could. And I did. It wasn't even much of a struggle. The thing is, when you set your mind on a particular goal, your body and mind see that as the end point of your day and dole out your mental and physical resources accordingly. Arriving at Garrigill, my resources were depleted, but after the initial disappointment, half a pint of chocolate milk and a Mars Bar from the desperate little shop just down from the pub, I got back on my feet and headed down the path along the river. I won't pretend that it was much fun. I can't even remember much about what was probably a very attractive riverside walk. What I do remember, was my immense relief when I saw the Alston youth hostel sign on the wall, right at the edge of town.

I checked in, dumped my gear in my room, changed my footwear and headed straight for the nearest pub. Never has a pint (I think it was Yates) tasted so good. Never has a bag of Pork Scratchings hit the spot so well.

A Lazy Day Along the Railway
Then on to The Wall

It was chilly in Alston the next morning as I sat eating a breakfast of milk, bread and cheese on a bench outside the Co-op. Here was a town I could live near; not too big, not too touristy and surrounded by great country. So what if it gets cut off by snow from time to time, that just adds to the allure.

From a quick look at my map, I could see that the Pennine Way roughly paralleled the abandoned railway now adopted by the South Tyne Trail, yet seemed to describe a gratuitously meandering route further up the valley side. After the exertions of the previous day, I was feeling lazy. A nice gentle stroll along a level rail bed on soft cinder seemed ideal – at least as far as the viaduct at Lambley. And I absolutely had to pass through Slaggyford; yet another nondescript cluster of stone houses with a world-beater of a name.

As you may have gathered by now, I didn't feel as though I was under any obligation to anyone to follow every inch of the Pennine Way. There are undoubtedly 'anoraks' (or as the motorcycle world would describe them, 'rivet-counters') who would feel as though they (or I) had somehow cheated by not following the signed path precisely. Everyone walks their own path. Mine led me astray from time to time and that was fine by me.

The amble along the disused railway was a welcome break, punctuated by the excitement of encountering some 'wildlife of unusual size' – rudimentary wood carvings that had been left at intervals along the route. After a while, the cinder gave way to grass, which made the walking even more relaxing and peaceful. The weather was fine and warm. I was having a glorious morning.

Eventually I reached the Lambley Viaduct, which is an impressive piece of 19th century civil engineering spanning the South Tyne River. Unfortunately the owner of the former station – now converted to a dwelling - had somewhat spoiled the experience by mean-spiritedly forcing walkers to drop down to the foot of the viaduct, then laboriously climb back up the other side, just to keep their little patch private. Englishmen. Castles. It's possible to take it all a bit too seriously.

After the easy walking of the morning, the last few miles across the moors to Greenhead were effortless. I had made it to Hadrian's Wall. Nevertheless, when I got to the village I went straight in to the Greenhead Hotel to see if they had a room. I had been carrying my sleeping bag and hammock for about 150 miles by this point but had only used them a handful of times. Perhaps I was getting soft. In my defence, the cool air, the wind and the steady effort of walking dragged most of the energy out of me by the end of the day, and a warm bed, a good meal and a pint or two were far more appealing than a chilly night out on the moors. While my hammock is a wonderful thing where there are trees to hang it from, suitable trees were few and far between and it makes a lousy tent. I was becoming a credit card hiker.

The Greenhead Hotel was able to accommodate me in a rather nice room above the bar. After a shower, an early supper and catching up with a bit of world news on the TV, I went to bed early.

At Hadrian's Wall, the Pennine Way turns abruptly east, following the wall for a few miles. It was raining hard in the morning and for some reason I was having a hard time relating what I could see on the ground with the lines and symbols on the map. What I interpreted as part of Magnis Roman Fort was some other massive earthwork. Before long, I was off track, north of the wall, struggling through a sheep pasture with a scruffy looking guy on a 4-wheeler bearing down on me. I was sure I was in for a tongue-lashing. His sheep-shit and mud stained rain coat was tied together with a baling twine belt. He looked as though he had been out in the rain for hours. His thin grey hair was plastered to his scalp, despite the hat which had long ago given up the struggle with the rain.

"Are you looking for Hadrian's Wall?" I said I was, and apologized for straying on to his land.

"Oh don't worry about that – happens all the time. Where are you from?"

Fortunately he was simply curious, perhaps a bit lonely and had clearly picked up on my foreignness as soon as the first words escaped my mouth. When people say looks can be deceiving, they must have had this gentleman in mind. As we chatted it became clear that he was erudite and well travelled – not at all the farm bumpkin I'd initially assumed. Not only had he been to Canada many times, he knew my local town well, describing elements of the down-town with accuracy and enthusiasm.

As the rain lashed down, our conversation ranged widely. I wasn't in the slightest bit bored and could happily have talked to him for hours, but he seemed completely oblivious to the rain which, by now had begun to seep through my second rate rain pants, soaking me above the knees. Finally I found tactful way to move on. He pointed me in the right direction, waved good-bye and set off to locate some of his sheep, while I squelched back to the path.

Although I'd been through a few showers and experienced plenty of cold and wind since leaving Edale, I hadn't experienced any serious rain days – until this one. It seemed somehow appropriate to be walking along the wall in the cold and wet. Other than a single elderly lady, who asked me to guess her age and got an honest, if disconcerting answer, there were no other hikers around and I was free to amble around the mile-castles and turrets at my leisure. A bit of rain was a small price to pay.

Just past the road to Haltwhistle, a group of scuba divers were getting all kitted up to dive in small, water-filled former quarry. At first I found it a bit ridiculous until it occurred to me that they might be training for more serious work.

Past the quarry, the wall climbs on to the top of the Whin Sill – the classic section of Hadrian's Wall, as featured in just about every promotional photograph and guide book. It's high, open and a bit remote. One can easily imagine a Roman guard, used to the warmer climate of Spain or Romania, shivering on his watch as he kept an eye out for invading Picts. I was keeping an eye out for a footpath leading to Twice Brewed pub and the chance for a lunchtime pint – perhaps to be accompanied by a morsel of something solid.

When I was in my early twenties I had hitch-hiked up to the wall, camped at the shore of Crag Lough, a little further to the east, then as dusk fell, had walked back along the wall to the Twice Brewed pub. Some considerable time later, with clumsy steps, I staggered back in the darkness. I spent what seemed like hours stomping around, trying to find my tent, finally locating it by tripping full length over a guy string. Oh the foolish things we do when we are young.

But none of that nonsense now. I just had a lunchtime refresher and some food, before ambling back to the wall. The Pennine Way leaves Hadrian's Wall just before Housesteads Roman Fort, heading north across boggy farm land before entering Wark Forest. In the pub, I had chatted briefly with a group of off-road motorbike riders. I had assumed they were heading down some farm track or other, so I was deeply annoyed to see that they had been ripping up the grass along the Pennine Way and had left every gate open behind them. Prats!

I like motorbikes – I have four of them and do a lot of long distance riding in Canada – but I don't like ignorant people who have no respect for farmers, who damage the countryside and can't keep off hiking trails.

The sterile plantations of Wark Forest did nothing for me at all. The Pennine Way just cuts across a small corner of the forest, but that was more than enough for me. Those bike riders had made me grumpy. I carried them with me while I plodded along the gravel roads and forest tracks until I reached the other side. As the day wore on, the rain subsided and the sky cleared leaving nothing but puddles, damp vegetation and a gentle haze to remember the rain. I slung my hammock from a couple of trees, within sight of open country. There wasn't much food left in my pack; an end of cheese, a couple of Hobnobs, a mouthful of water, but Bellingham was just five miles further north. I would re-supply in the morning. That night, I slept like a baby. Nothing induces sleep better than a gently swaying hammock, cool air and a tired body. If I stirred during the night, I certainly don't remember it.

Bellingham and Beyond

I was up, packed and on the move by about 6 0'clock. The map showed that the walk to Bellingham wouldn't be particularly testing although some of the names on the map caught my eye. I soon passed Horneystead, followed, after a couple of miles, by Brownsleazes, perhaps an outpost of Shitlington Hall, before clambering up Shitlington Crags and the descent towards Bellingham.

As I walked along the road into the village I saw two heavily loaded hikers heading my way. My guess is that they were in their late teens or early twenties. We stopped to chat and they said they had been intending to walk the whole Pennine Way but if their expressions were anything to go by, they were about to give up.

They had started off from Kirk Yetholm a few days earlier but bad weather and, I suspect, the unexpected level of effort, had forced them to overnight in one of the two mountain refuge huts in the Cheviots. From the way they described it, the rest of their journey had been no picnic either. I tried to encourage them by suggesting that they had already done the hard part. It would be nice to think they carried on, but I doubt whether they did.

I had to wait for a while before the grocery store in Bellingham opened. Once again, it was a Co-op, offering a fine assortment of the staples of this dedicated long distance hiker. I had another fourteen miles of boggy moor and forest track to walk before I reached Byrness and needed plenty of sustaining treats to carry me along.

Bellingham to Byrness was the final run-up to the Cheviots. In the morning, I would either have to walk the whole twenty-six miles along the crest of the Cheviot Hills to Kirk Yetholm, or chicken out and break the trip at one of the huts. At nineteen miles, this day was just a warm up.

By the time I got to the private hostel at Byrness I was tired. I tried to imagine having to walk another seven miles but couldn't. My legs wanted a bed, my stomach wanted food, my mind wanted beer. I got all three. The warden showed me my bed – a narrow bunk in a small room – and whipped me up a curry. It may have been frozen once and the rice may have been industrial, but I didn't care, it went down really well. Best of all, he had a cabinet full of various beers for me to sample. I would need those extra calories if I was going to survive the last leg.

I've done my fair share of whining about being tired at the end of the day and it's all true. It's a natural consequence of walking fairly good distances, carrying a pack over rough terrain in all kinds of weathers. By this point in a long distance hike, one's body has either completely rebelled, or has reached a point of equilibrium, so that the next day is 'just another day at the office'. It's not that you don't feel the aches and pains, don't feel tired at the end of the day, don't struggle to get up that infernal slope, don't feel the weight of the pack digging into shoulders and hips, it's just that it all becomes so routine that it's no longer a bother. Feet? I'd long ago stopped worrying about them and given up any pretence of trying to keep them dry. They'd settled in nicely; no hot spots, no blisters, no aches and pains, regardless whether they were wet or dry all day.

The Best Bath Ever

I must have been tired. Usually I wake up early, choke down something for breakfast then get moving as soon as possible. This day though, I wasn't moving until just before eight. The path led up a steep, 650 foot climb from the valley to Byrness Hill through thick plantation forest, ending in a jumble of big boulders close to the tree line. A sign near the top welcomed me to the 'Otterburn Ranges' – a major Ministry of Defence military shooting range, with limited public access. Fortunately, there is no firing near the route of the Pennine Way and I didn't hear a single shot all day, for which I was quite thankful.

I could already feel that I was going to enjoy this day. The route follows a high ridge, along the spine of the Cheviot Hills, which also forms the border between Scotland and England for most of the way. The weather was cool and overcast with little wind – perfect walking weather. Although the distance was a bit intimidating, I knew that there were two mountain refuge huts along the route which could be used in a pinch. I don't think my mind was fully committed to the whole distance when I set out. As usual, I had decided that I would see what transpired and deal with it accordingly.

The path was little more than a slightly flattened and worn trough in the surrounding vegetation. In some areas it was a bit soggy but for the first few miles at least, the going was reasonably firm and the weather was cooperating. I got the distinct impression that this part of the Pennine Way doesn't see as much use as some of the others. Perhaps the distance puts people off, or the limited opportunities for baling out, making a circuit, or finding a pub. Perhaps names like 'Windy Crag' and 'Ogre Hill' dissuade a timid few. Whatever the reasons, I was content to be swinging along, feeling good. That there was no-one else about just made it more enjoyable. Despite the overcast sky, I could see the hills extending off in all directions and it felt quite remote. There were a few patches of snow in the hollows, but nothing that looked as though it would impede my travel.

I reached the Roman camp at Chew Green far sooner than I expected. The earthworks were visible from some distance, enclosing a large area within their banks and ditches. I had a brief rest on the top of one of the banks, before heading up to the old signal station past Brownhart Law. This was gentle ridge walking at its best. The up-hills weren't too steep, the down-hills were kind to my knees and the footing was good. Perhaps that's a slight exaggeration. In places the route traversed level ground where there was almost as much water at the surface as vegetation, so I sloshed through them, no longer bothering to try to keep my feet dry. I was sloshing through one particularly damp section when my eye suddenly caught some movement. The feral goats of the Cheviots are thought to be remnants of creatures imported to Britain during the Neolithic period, about 5000 years ago. They certainly look the part with shaggy, dark brown and blotchy grey hair and short horns, their wild appearance fits the landscape perfectly and it's easy to tell that a bit of cold and wet wouldn't bother them at all.

I had kept the mountain refuge hut at Lamb Hill in my mind as a possible place to stay if the weather got truly foul but I reached it far to early in the day to think about stopping. From the outside it was rather attractive, with ship-lap wood siding and a sloping roof. The inside was another matter; just bare plywood walls, benches around the sides and a few bits and pieces left by previous travellers. I would have to be really desperate to want to spend the night there. I thought of the two lads I'd met in Bellingham. It can't have been much fun for them. No wonder they were thinking about quitting if they thought it would all be that tough.

The map indicated that it was about 9 miles along the ridge to the next mountain refuge hut at Auchope Rig. The weather was with me, my body was holding up fine – let's go! Part of this section had been slabbed, making the walking effortless and pleasant, nevertheless, it was still a longish way, punctuated by cairns, hill tops and an elevation that never dropped below 1500 feet.

On the audio clip which accompanies the photo of 'Windy Gyle', all you can hear is the sound of the wind and me saying "It certainly lives up to its name".

As the day wore on, the wind did indeed pick up, blowing away some of the low cloud and exposing a bit of blue sky between the grey. I pressed on past multiple cairns and over Butt Roads, King's Seat, Score Head and Crookedsike Head then past the side path up to the top of The Cheviot. I didn't feel like adding an extra two miles to my day, just to be able to say I was on its top, so I gave it a miss and headed down the slope to the second rescue hut.

Auchope Rig hut sits on a broad shoulder with The Cheviot to the east and the valley containing the hamlet of Sourhope to the west. Sometimes you just have to wonder how some of these place names originated, but in this instance the name actually is an accurate reflection of the location. Apparently the settlement, which has its origins in the 14th century, was named for the 'valley of sour pastures'. Research in the 1970's determined that the soils in the area are deficient in copper and cobalt which accounts for the 'sourness'.

The hut was virtually identical to the first one. I didn't bother to go inside because the wind had finally blown most of the clouds away – for a while at least – and the bench outside was bathed in sunlight. My supply of reserve food was at a low ebb, but I found a Mars Bar and I still had some water in my bottle for a small drink, so I sat on the bench and watched the remaining clouds race across the sky. It's conventional wisdom that mountain weather is changeable. This is one piece of wisdom that holds true. While I was slowly warming in the sun's rays an ominously dark cloud was blowing in from the north and seemed to loiter over Black Hag. I quickly stowed my gear, hoisted my pack and got moving. Predictably, the path to Kirk Yetholm and the end of the journey meant heading straight for the cloud.

It didn't take long before I was surrounded, the tops of the hills disappeared and a mixture of snow and rain blew horizontally across the slopes. I was a bit fearful that such a dark cloud might produce lightning. A sole hiker on an exposed ridge is an attractive target for Zeus's arrows. As the snow raced by, a rainbow curved up from the valley, it's upper end lost in the darkness above. Then, almost as soon as it had appeared, it vanished, and along with it, the cloud and snow. The hills were visible again.

I quickly climbed over The Schil then started the descent to the shoulder between it and Black Hag. The Pennine Way bifurcates at Black Hag; one route descending into the Halter Burn valley then along a farm track to Kirk Yetholm; the other follows further along the ridge past White Law before taking a more direct path to the village. I took the low road. I won't try to pretend that I wasn't tired. Those last five miles from Black Hag to the village were easy walking, but my legs had started to turn to jelly, especially by the time I hit the paved road with about a mile to go. It was now well into the evening and beginning to get dark.

The buildings of Kirk Yetholm are spaced around a broad central green. I had heard that there was a Youth Hostel in the village, but I was too tired to go hunting for it. I headed straight for the Border Hotel – the official end of the Pennine Way.

If I had been expecting some kind of welcoming; perhaps a brawny, kilted Scotsman slapping me on the back, saying,

"Walked the Pennine Way have ye laddie, well done – here, have a pint", I would have been sorely disappointed. I walked in to the hotel bar, put my rucksack in the corner and ordered a pint. There was hardly anyone around and those that were had no interest in me. The guy behind the bar sorted a room for me and once I finished my drink, led me upstairs, through convoluted passageways to a nicely appointed single room. It had all the necessaries: a big fluffy bed, a flat screen TV, and in the bathroom, a huge, deep bathtub. I have had many fine baths, in many

Actually, I'm English

different places, but of all the wonderful baths I've had, the one in the Border Hotel will remain in my memory as the 'best bath ever'. It was deep. It was long. It was wide, and the hot water was endless. I filled the tub, settled in and could immediately feel all those long, weary miles melting away.

My trip to the UK wasn't quite over. From Kirk Yetholm, I caught a series of buses to Langholm, just north of Carlisle, where I rented a Royal Enfield motorbike for another two weeks of bodily abuse, visiting friends and relatives all over the UK. During the 2500 miles of the motorbike journey, I experienced cold and wet beyond even what the Pennines could throw at me.

Pennine Way

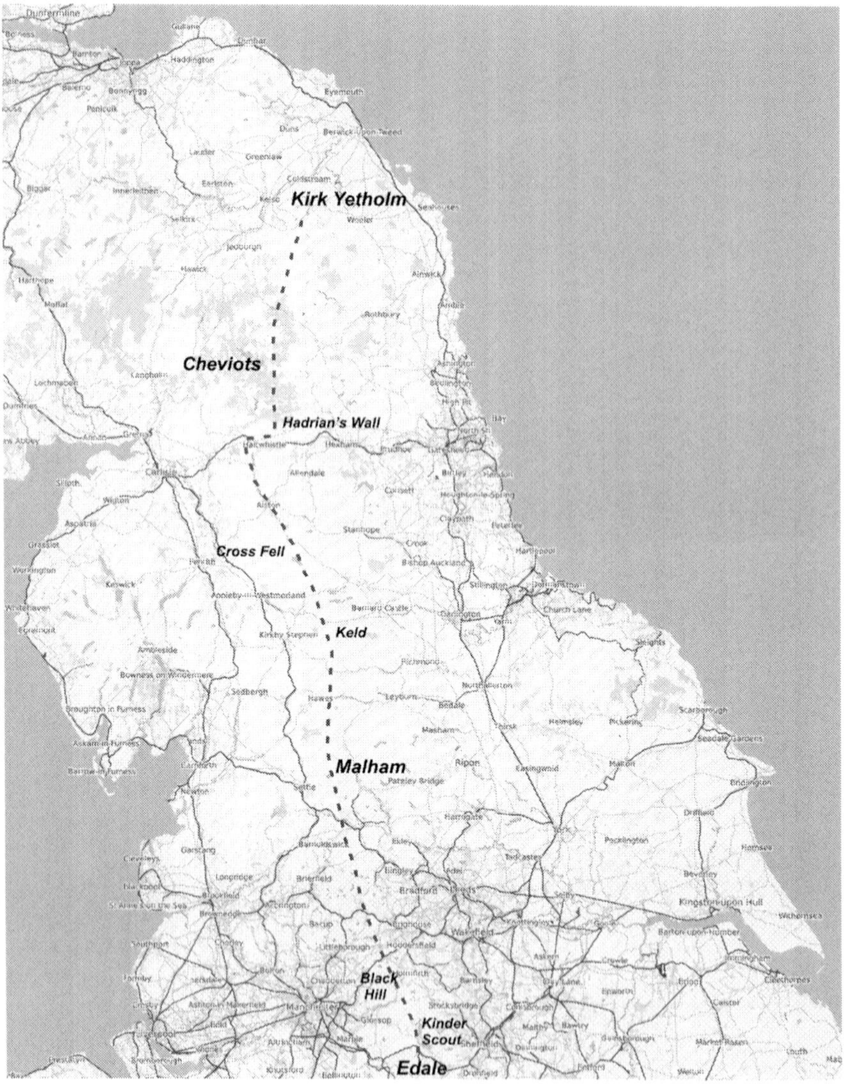
Kirk Yetholm
Cheviots
Hadrian's Wall
Cross Fell
Keld
Malham
Black Hill
Kinder Scout
Edale

Actually, I'm English

On Kinder Scout

Looking for beer mats

Pen-y-ghent from Fountains Fell

morning near Bellingham

PART 3

AROUND ENGLAND BY ROYAL ENFIELD
Langholm to York

I should have known that my hiking gear wouldn't be much use on the motorbike; it took less than an hour of riding for it to become obvious that I was going to be woefully under dressed for the next two weeks. People had warned me that riding in Britain in March might be a bit chilly, but I hadn't been prepared to listen.

After spending the previous couple of weeks hiking I was feeling vigorous and robust. My rain gear had been tested through innumerable rain and hail showers. I was ready for anything.

Everything was going according to plan. After a pleasant night at the Border Hotel, I awoke feeling refreshed, gulped down a quick plate of bacon and eggs and prepared myself for the next leg of my trip. The single decker bus which plies the route between Kelso and Galashields is far too wide for the narrow, twisty roads, but the young lady driver handled it with the skill and speed of a rally driver. The second leg of the bus journey to Langholm was a bit more sedate and I was deposited in the middle of the delightful village, just before lunchtime.

While searching the web for motorbike rental places in the UK, I had stumbled upon A7 Motorcycles, who, at that time, rented bikes and conducted tours throughout northern England and the Highlands. With Langholm being only a couple of short bus rides away from the end of the Pennine Way, it seemed a perfect fit.

Although other rental places offered a wide variety of modern motorcycles to choose from, it was the Enfield that really appealed to me. The latest version of the Royal Enfield Bullet 500 boasts a redesigned 'lean burn' long-stroke engine, modern fuel injection and a front disk brake. Other than these concessions to modernity, I had read that it retained the look, feel and economy of the earlier bikes, but with slightly better performance and decidedly better stopping power. I couldn't wait to find out for myself.

Langholm to York

A7 Motorcycles have a small shop front on the main road, almost directly across the street from where the bus dropped me. The bike I would be using was sitting ready in the middle of the showroom; a lovely rich, cherry red Royal Enfield 500 with less than 3000 miles on the clock, with a robust rear rack and a large set of saddlebags. Within a few minutes the owners, Helen and Jonathan had welcomed me, gone over the bike with me, completed all the paperwork, equipped me with a helmet and gloves, found a place in their shop to store the camping equipment I wouldn't be needing and wheeled the bike out to the road ready for departure.

It didn't take long to fill the panniers, strap my rucksack to the rack and dress myself ready for the road. After a quick spin around a parking lot to get the feel of the bike, I felt confident enough to head south, making sure to take off on the left side of the road. At idle, the Enfield chuffed quietly through its enormous silencer. As I accelerated up to traffic speed, the note changed in volume and tone, but never managed the ear shattering roar of classic British bikes of the fifties and sixties. It was muted; positively civilized.

The A7 leads south from Langholm towards Carlisle and is a fast main road, so I had no alternative but to accelerate up to the ambient road speed and join the main traffic flow for a while. I was pleasantly surprised at how punchy the Bullet felt, pulling strongly up to 60mph with little apparent effort. Compared to the larger and heavier motorcycles I ride in Canada, it felt light and responsive, although without a windscreen and with an upright riding position, I was soon feeling the wind on my arms and chest. I was happy to leave the main road for slower and less heavily travelled byways.

I had arranged to stay with friends in York that night. It is only about 135 miles from Langholm to York - a distance that seemed entirely manageable, even after an early afternoon start. The route I planned weaved its way south-east, passing through Barnard Castle and avoiding as many main roads as possible.

Within half an hour I started to feel the cold. My boots were still damp from my slog across the Cheviots and the cold was seeping up from my feet and chilling the rest of me. I pulled in to a field entrance, changed my socks and added another layer beneath my rain jacket.

At Barnard Castle, since everyone else seemed to park there, I rode up on to the cobbled strip in the middle of Market Place and parked the bike. I needed two things: a bathroom, which I found just off Horse Market, and a couple of sausage rolls to give my depleted stomach something to work on. Like a cow or a goat, as long as my innards are churning away on something, I tend to stay warm.

I should have had four sausage rolls. An hour later, it was pitch black, pouring with rain and I was unsure as to whether I was heading in the right direction. Water had worked its way through my jacket. My arms and belly were soaked. My pants, which had been a perfect length for hiking, were riding up on my knees so that the cuffs ended just above my boots. As they shed the rain and the spray from the road, they cleverly directed it into my boots. The leather gloves which I had kindly been loaned by Helen and Jonathan were now completely wet, clammy and cold.

The Enfield's headlight cast a pool of light ahead on the narrow and twisty road. Everyone else seemed to have the good sense to stay inside. Traffic was light and I more-or-less had the road to myself. Despite my discomfort, I found myself grinning inside my helmet. What on earth did I think I was doing, riding a strange (to me) bike, in the middle of nowhere, on the wrong (for me) side of the road, in the kind of darkness that only a wet night in Britain can produce? I was wet, cold and a bit lost. What was I doing? I was having a whale of a time!

Soon enough I found some road signs which led me in the right direction. The rain was still coming down in sheets when I arrived in York and after riding around the town centre for a while, I gave up trying to find my friend's house by instinct and called them on the phone. It was one shivery drowned rat they welcomed into their house that night.

York to Norfolk

Warmed with copious quantities of wine and food and a pleasant sleep, I was completely restored when I set off for Norfolk next morning. Although my boots were still soggy, the rain had stopped and the temperature had risen a couple of degrees, making riding almost pleasant.

Its about 170 miles from York to my friends house in Norfolk. As before, I avoided main highways whenever I could, picking secondary roads through farming country. While this marginally increased the duration and distance of the ride, it exponentially increased my enjoyment. I crossed the Ouse at Goole, (which is far less interesting than it sounds), stopping briefly for a coffee break and the inevitable old bike chat with a passer by. The Enfield was running perfectly, the seat and riding position were comfortable and, for a while at least, my body temperature was neutral. I was starting to settle in.

As I rolled along between Sleaford and Swineshead, a policeman stepped in to the road and signalled for me to pull in to a lay-by.

"Good morning officer."

"Good morning sir. You weren't doing anything wrong - we're just doing roadside checks."

He asked me for my licence and insurance, which I dutifully produced. When I handed over my Ontario motorcycle licence, the look on his face was priceless. I almost expected him to say:

"Hello, hello, hello, what's all this 'ere then",

but he didn't, he just looked perplexed until I explained that I was on holiday and the motorcycle was rented from a company in Scotland.

Talking in the radio on his shoulder, it didn't take him long to corroborate my story, but to confuse him further, I then pulled out my British motorcycle licence (renewed last in 1983) and asked him if he could find out whether it was still valid. By now we were getting quite chummy, so he checked the number over the radio and confirmed that although the residency address wasn't any good any more, the licence was still valid until 2021. I bade him good day and rode off, mindful of the speed limit, of course, heading for Wisbech.

I've always liked Wisbech. There's not much to it; a small town centre, some rather nice Dutch influenced 18th century houses lining the tidal river, a slight but pervasive odour of wet mud and seaweed and some of the best fish and chips available anywhere. I parked the bike, bought some cod, chips and a coke from a chippy in the market square, found a spot on a bench and dug in.

The rest of the ride to my friends house in Norfolk was uneventful and I arrived to find Julia struggling at their gate with her arms full of a disturbing quantity of beer and liquor. Every time I'm in England, I spend two or three days with these friends and it always follows the same pattern. I arrive sometime in the afternoon. We start drinking and talking early. We continue until we've demolished the prodigious booze supply and started to work through whichever toxic home concoctions are in the cupboard or we can no longer talk, whichever comes sooner. You would think that after 40 years it would have become stale. It hasn't.

Rediscovering Norfolk

Before I left for Canada, I had spent a few years working in Norfolk. It was, and remains, a place I love. It's not that the scenery is outstanding, it isn't, but it has a special and distinctive rural charm. It's not even that I was born here, even though I was. No, it's that it is a little empty, a little quiet, a little peaceful – a bit of a backwater.

Back in the fourteenth century, it was one of the the richest and most heavily populated parts of the country. The business of raising sheep for wool brought money and people to the area. Norwich was the second largest city in England and the countryside was spotted with wealthy villages and lavishly decorated churches. The Black Death and subsequent plagues changed all that. Norfolk is one of the few parts of the UK where the population is still lower now than it was 600 years ago. Many villages are dwarfed by churches built for far more numerous parishioners. Some villages have disappeared altogether, now only visible as lumps and bumps in a field, perhaps surrounding a stump of flint rubble – all that remains of the church.

I had promised myself a ride up to the north Norfolk coast, visiting some of my favourite places on the way, so somewhat groggily, I wheeled the bike through the gate on to the road. As usual, the Enfield started instantly with the slightest push on the starter button. I was starting to approve of this bike.

My first stop was Castle Acre for the hair of the dog. Castle Acre is the perfect English village - at least, it is in my opinion. You enter the main village area through a mediaeval gate, the remnant of defensive works that enclosed the settlement, leading on to an elongated village green, lined by classic Norfolk flint and brick houses. There's a Norman motte and bailey castle, the remains of a once massive 12th century Clunaic Priory, and the 'Ostrich' pub - a 16th century brick and timber coaching inn. The River Nar runs below the village and the Roman 'Peddar's Way', probably following a much more ancient track-way passes close by.

While working in Norfolk I spent many happy hours with friends, converting my pay to urine in the bar at the Ostrich. The pub no longer caters to Norfolk rustics and now entices the BMW/Audi set, nevertheless, the building is undiminished and the beer is good. If the clientèle now smell more of Brut than brute sweat, that's a small price to pay to see the grand old pub continue. So many have closed in recent years.

After soaking in the ambiance of Caste Acre for a while, I headed north towards Holt then on to visit some of my favourite Saxon churches along the coast road.

The Royal Enfield Bullet was beginning to win my heart. Trickling along winding, hedgerow enclosed lanes, it was completely in its element. This is why bikes like this were made: steady, reliable, light, economical, with a mellifluous exhaust note - what could be better? The sun even deigned to shine, albeit with the weakness typical of March, and was largely devoid of warmth.

There are few tourists on Norfolk roads in March so it felt as though I had the countryside to myself. It's a spare world of brown tilled fields, leafless hedgerows interspersed with jagged oaks, flint pan-tiled cottages and brick garden walls. Some of the villages have a few modern houses around their fringes, but they retain the feel and character of an earlier time. Norfolk has no motorways. Once you are off the trunk roads radiating from Norwich, it is a county of minor roads and quiet places. Even the coast road, which can be a misery of traffic in the summer, was quiet, allowing me to tootle along at my own pace, stopping to visit round towered flint churches along the way. I stopped at Cley-next-the-Sea to take a picture of the windmill, then ambled on to Blakeney to look out across the broad expanse of tidal flats beyond the harbour before heading back to stay another night with my friends in Fransham. Distances in Norfolk aren't huge. Nevertheless, by the time I returned, I was well chilled and quite ready for a more restrained evening of drink and conversation in front of a warm coal fire.

Norfolk to Devon

The next leg of my journey involved a long haul down to Ashburton, Devon, in the shadow of Dartmoor. It was a 300+ mile slog diagonally across southern England, which may not sound like much of a ride to North Americans, but let me tell you, in Britain, that can be a long, hard day. My main desire was to skirt London and to avoid as many town centres as I could, although main roads were somewhat inevitable if I was ever to get there in one day.

Nevertheless, despite the busier roads, I did quite enjoy myself. Once again, the bike performed flawlessly, purring along comfortably while consuming very little fuel. While certainly not the fastest thing on the road, the Enfield had enough power and speed to avoid being an impediment to other road users. I didn't venture on the motorway system yet.

My route across southern England followed the same basic orientation as the prehistoric Icknield Way, along the edge of the

Cretaceous chalk escarpment which extends from north Norfolk to Salisbury Plain in Wiltshire. I skirted Cambridge, passed through the wonderfully named Leighton Buzzard, then on to Wallingford, Andover and Honiton, before reaching Ashburton late in the day. To be perfectly honest, I can't remember much of that day. It was a blur of small towns and villages, low, rolling hills, traffic, diesel fumes and hedgerows.

Ashburton is a delightful little town, its main buildings strung out along West Street - the road between Exeter and Plymouth. I slowly cruised through the town then parked the bike in the little lane which leads to the 15th century St. Andrew's Church. I knew from looking at Google Streetview that my old school friend John lived more-or-less opposite the church in a three story town-house right on the main street.

John was home. The bike was soon safely parked in his workshop, meals were eaten, wine was consumed. Over the next couple of days it rained solidly. Nevertheless we canoed on the River Dart, hiked on part of the South-west Coast Path, got completely soaked and exchanged lies and tall tales like old friends.

Time was, unfortunately, starting to run out so I said my goodbyes and headed north. My original idea had been to buckle down and complete the 450 miles back to Langholm in a single day, but nature had other plans.

Devon to Langholm – Part 1

It was raining when I left John's place, so instead of heading straight for the road north, I stopped at a farm supply store to beef up my riding gear with an industrial strength, day-glow workman's jacket and some heavy nylon rain pants. Foolishly I didn't think about my hands and feet as I was still warm from a substantial breakfast and my boots and gloves were completely dry.

It didn't take me long to realise my mistake. The rain kept coming down. Within minutes my gloves were a soggy mess and my hands were starting to get uncomfortably cold. My new rain gear was doing a great job of keeping my body protected, but it seemed as though every drop of moisture shed by the suit ended up draining straight into my boots. I'm generally quite resistant to the cold, but with the temperature hovering just above the freezing point and hard rain battering down, I hadn't travelled many miles before I was seriously chilled.

I pulled into a garage to fill the Enfield's fuel tank and was able to buy a roll of duct tape which I used to seal the junction between my rain pants and my boots. This helped a little, but of course, by this point my feet were so cold that keeping further water out made little difference. The duct tape added little to the aesthetic appeal of my ensemble, but there were few to see.

The only good thing I have to say about that day's ride was that the Royal Enfield continued to hum along apparently unbothered by the cold and wet. The same could not be said for me. My hands were becoming so numb that I started having difficulty holding on to the handlebars. My fingers felt three times their normal size. Manipulating the clutch and the front brake was decidedly awkward.

In one of the small towns - it might have been Illchester, but I wasn't really in a condition to notice or care by this point - I found a clothing store that sold work gloves. Two thin pairs of wool gloves just about fit into bright orange rubber over-gloves - you know the type - the ones sanitation engineers have in their toolbox but never bother to use. It was the best I could come up with.

With my hands gradually thawing, all my attention reverted to my feet which by now felt giant and weirdly spongy. The cold was moving steadily up my legs and my knees were beginning to seize up. By the time I'd ridden the 137 miles to Swindon, I'd had enough. But I had a plan!

Once I'd had a chance to jam some food down, which did little to alleviate the pervasive cold which by now had taken a complete hold of my body, I started looking for car rental places. I thought that if I could rent a van or truck, I could deliver the bike back to Langholm, all the while sitting in the delicious warmth of the cab. Perfect!

It didn't take long for my hopes to be dashed. The first rental place I tried didn't have any suitable vehicles available. The next two wouldn't rent to a foreigner with an Ontario licence and no fixed abode in the UK. Disappointed, I dragged my shivering body back on to the bike and carried on. 35 miles later, a sodden, shaking, frozen and perhaps a little incoherent motorcyclist wandered into the vestibule at the Stow-on-the-Wold Youth Hostel.

That evening I spent a rather long time thawing out in the Queen's Head in the market square. The food was plentiful and the beer was suitably numbing. Eventually I wandered back to the youth hostel. There were only two other people sharing my room. I must have out-snored them, as I had an excellent and restorative sleep.

Devon to Langholm – Part 2

Despite all the tales I had heard about the abundance of petty theft in the UK, the bike was still where I had left it the previous evening. Clearly nobody thought taking a motorcycle for a joy ride in this weather was a good idea. Before throwing the bags and rucksack on the bike, I did a quick systems check. The oil level was still good, there were no nasty drips staining the municipal pavement and the tyres had plenty of air. The chain was rather loose though, so I unpacked the tool-kit from the toolbox and set to. For some reason the tool kit didn't include anything to fit the wheel nuts, but I was able to borrow one from the youth hostel maintenance guy. Within ten or fifteen minutes I was on the road and heading for Scotland again.

The rain had stopped, the skies had cleared, and while it would be stretching the truth to say that it was warm, at least it wasn't dangerously cold. As before, I opted to eschew major highways, sticking to less well travelled 'A' and some 'B' roads, passing by or through Evesham, Kidderminster, Bridgenorth, and Whitchurch before heading into the more industrial landscapes of Warrington and Wigan.

I'm not sure whether it was because of my increased confidence in the bike, or my desire to pick up the pace a bit, but after Wigan, I joined the M6 motorway for the long haul through Lancashire along the western edge of the Pennines. British motorways have a speed limit of 70 miles per hour, so of course most people travel around 80. I had no intention of thrashing the Enfield at those speeds and settled in comfortably between 60 and 65, along with the most heavily laden lorrys, old Bedford camper vans and geriatric grannies in Nissan Micras.

In typical orderly British fashion (or so the mythology goes, at least), faster vehicles pass on the right and nobody passes on the left, so while riding a motorbike at slower than ambient traffic speeds isn't all that advisable, it isn't actually all that dangerous either. You are not likely to get some crazed speeder suddenly switching to the left lane to manoeuvre past a sluggish pantechnicon. That may happen in less civilized countries, but in Britain? Never!

By the time I left the M6 and headed in to the town of Kendal at the southern edge of the Lake District, the cold had seeped back into my bones, so I was happy to encounter a whole string of B&B's on the road in to town. I chose one, knocked on the door and was quickly ushered in by the landlady who clearly thought I was a bit demented. Before even showing me my room, she made me a cup of tea and pointed to where I could safely park the bike on her patio at the rear of the house. The bed was comfortable, the room was warm, restaurants were a short walk away and best of all, it was dirt cheap. Content in Kendal!

I hadn't expected the trip from Devon to Langholm to take three days, but this was the only pace my body would allow. By the end of each day my reserves of stamina and body heat were entirely exhausted and no matter how warm the pub or bedroom, I would continue to shiver well into the night.

From Kendal to Langholm is a mere 70 miles, so, after getting some fuel for both me and the bike, I set off north again. On leaving Kendal, the road rises almost immediately, crossing the shoulder of Shap Fell and reaching a maximum elevation of 1400ft (435 metres), which doesn't sound like much until you consider the weather which races in from the Irish Sea. Until the construction of the M6, the A6 over Shap used to be the main road between England and Scotland, a route that was legendary for brutal winter weather. Fortunately for me, the sun was shining, so even if there was a bit of frost on the road and I had to watch for black ice, Shap was being relatively benign.

The last few miles have become a blur and no specific events or memories stand out. I arrived in Langholm, deposited the bike with A7, settled up, retrieved my gear, caught a bus to Carlisle and a train back to York and a comfortable bed back with my friends.

If there's a lesson to be learned from this brief adventure, its that gear which is perfectly suitable for hiking is completely inadequate on a motorbike. Before I started riding the Enfield, I had been hiking and rough-camping through snow storms, sub-zero temperatures and icy wind and rain. While I experienced plenty of cold, at no time did I come even remotely close to being as cold as I was while riding the bike.

Perhaps a secondary cautionary note should be that while the weather in Britain doesn't usually reach the extremes experienced in some other countries, it can still throw up conditions punishing to the human body. I was probably borderline hypothermic some of the time - a condition which not only saps the strength, but enfeebles the mind. It must have done, because if I ask myself whether I would do it again, the answer is "of course I would". Perhaps even, "of course I will", only this time with slightly better gear.

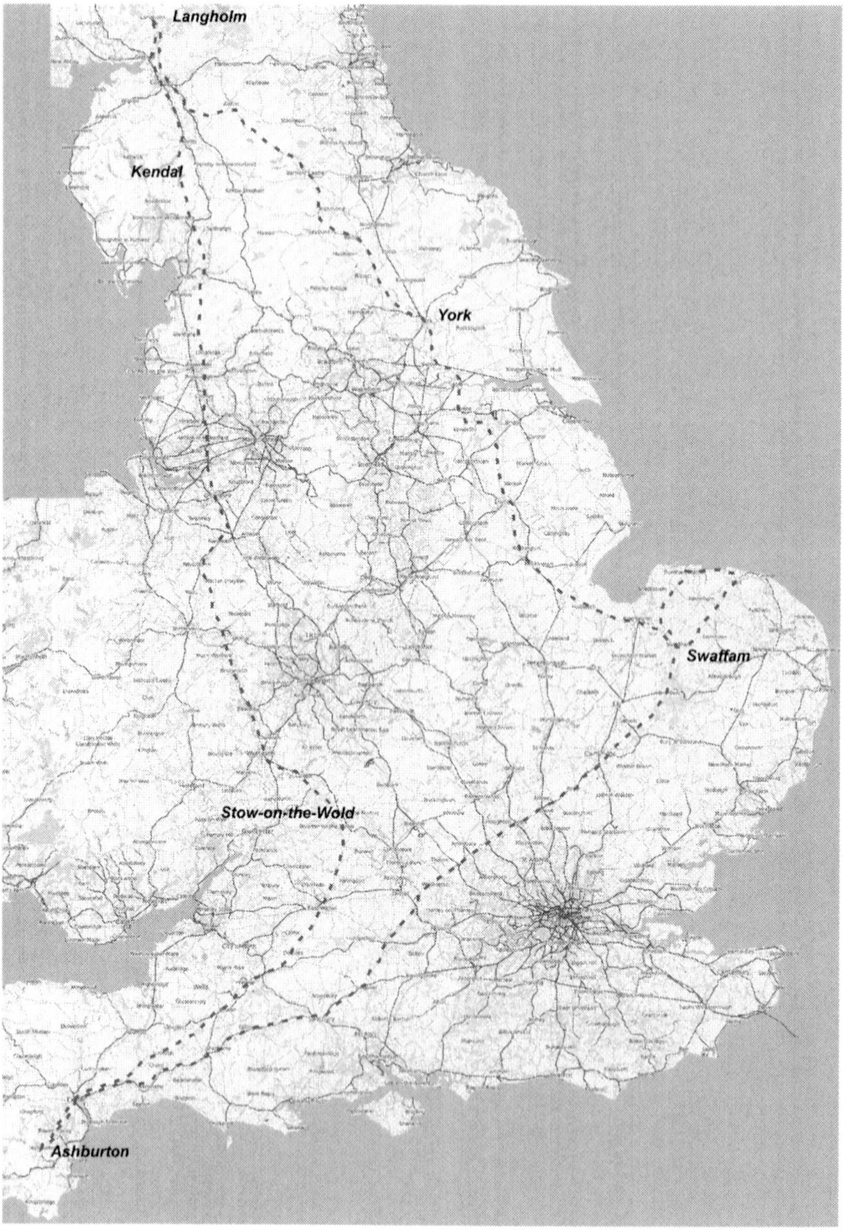
Langholm
Kendal
York
Swaffam
Stow-on-the-Wold
Ashburton

Great Massingham, Norfolk

On Shap

PART 4

BITS AND PIECES
- WALES, PEAK DISTRICT, LAKES -

Chepstow to Welshpool

The winter of 2013 was brutal. By February I was chafing to do something more interesting and energetic than sitting all day in my basement office watching the snow fall. A quick check on-line showed that I could get a direct flight between Ottawa and Heathrow for a good price at short notice. In a matter of days, I was in the departure lounge at the airport, watching the snow sifting down, wondering whether my flight would be able to take off.

Ottawa is used to snow. No cancellations were showing on the departures board and as I watched, a peleton of snow-ploughs made its way across the runway while the wings of our plane were de-iced. Within minutes we boarded and in no time we were powering into the dark, grey sky.

My hastily conceived plan for this year was to start in Chepstow, walk up Offa's Dyke as far as Welshpool, follow the Montgomery and Llangollen Canals to Whitchurch, walk across to the foot of the Pennines on the South Cheshire Way, then head north, following the Limestone and Pennine Ways as far as Reeth. From Reeth, I intended to walk west on the Coast to Coast Path through the Lake District, to end up at St. Bees. It didn't work out that way.

At first everything went wonderfully. Once I had retrieved my rucksack, I followed the signs for the buses. In less than half an hour, I was on a bus heading to Chepstow from Heathrow, happily watching the fields slip by as we sped along the M4. I know it's a bit of a tradition to complain about the British transportation system, but it never ceases to amaze me how easily and relatively cheaply one can zip from one part of the country to the next, only waiting a few chilly, damp minutes in unheated terminals between connections. The bus dropped me just up the street from a grocery store where I was able to get some survival basics before heading past the castle to find my way to Offa's Dyke.

I'd first walked Offa's Dyke in 2006, so I knew where I was going. The Offa's Dyke path is a 177 mile long National Trail which more-or-less follows the route of the eighth century earthwork after which it's named. In the days leading up to my flight from Ottawa to Heathrow, I had been reading the UK flood reports with increasing perturbation. I wondered whether some of the low-lying sections of the path would even be passable. I'm glad I decided to take the chance. As luck would have it, the generally low temperatures meant that many of the most muddy areas had a nice firm, frosty crust, which made those mucky areas quite easy to traverse.

I walked past the castle, across the muddy and tidal River Wye on the upstream bridge, then on to the path which roughly follows the river all the way to Monmouth. I had taken a different route out of Chepstow on the previous hike; this one took me right by the towering walls of the castle. Attacking a castle like Chepstow much have been a daunting task. It was easy to imagine hot buckets of oil and excrement being thrown from the walls and arrows zinging from the narrow slits.

In order to avoid the villages of Tutshill and Woodcroft, the path sticks close to the top of the cliff above the river, in places sandwiched between people's back gardens and a rather unnerving drop. This section is heavily forested. In places, and despite the trees, it was easy to tell that you were walking on Offa's actual bank, with the ditch immediately below; in others the path diverts from the dyke, presumably to preserve delicate sections.

In some places, the path had been rehabilitated with pea gravel and lined by marker stones. At first I found this new work rather intrusive and unsettling until I realised that nature would reclaim it soon enough and the well marked path would quickly blend with the surrounding woods.

At the Devil's Pulpit look-out, you can look down on to the ruins of Tintern Abbey on the floodplain below. A quick check of my map showed that I had two options. I could either follow the main path and the dyke, up through St. Briavels Common or take a lower route down to the pub at Brockweir. Not a difficult choice! I'd already been on the move for about 30 hours by this point. A quick pint in a rustic English pub would be just the ticket.

Instead of finding an intersecting path, I just headed straight down the valley edge, through the woods in the general direction of the village. After about five minutes of thrashing through the undergrowth, stepping over fallen branches and avoiding huge beech trees, I noticed a large figure ahead of me, standing silently looking out of the valley. I took a few more steps, but not wishing to surprise the chap in case he was in some kind of trance, I called out 'hello'.

Fergus (I'll call him Fergus because of his big, shaggy beard) turned to see me stomping down the slope in his direction.

"Sorry to disturb you," I said, "but I thought it would be rude to barge past without even saying hello".

"Oh that's OK. Virtually nobody ever leaves the path, so I was a bit surprised to see you. I was just enjoying the view. What part of the States are you from?"

"Actually........................"

We had a long and very pleasant conversation about hiking, travel and motorbikes. Fergus had lived in California for a while and had spent some time there as a motorbike mechanic before his visitor visa ran out. I was enjoying listening to him talk - he had a wonderful local accent, full of mellow vowels and an abundance of r's – and clearly loved his part of the world.

Fergus pointed me in the direction of Brockweir. As I gained the lower footpath I looked back up the slope. He was still there, staring out across the river.

The Brockweir Country Inn has managed to retain much of it's rural charm and does not seem to done much to pander to the substantial summertime trade of hikers and tourists it must experience. I parked my rucksack on the bench outside and wandered in. There were only a couple of other people in the bar, probably locals, quietly nursing their drinks. The barman served me a pint and sold me a bag of crisps, but since there was no other food available and the light was starting to fade, I didn't tarry long.

I had already decided where I would sleep that night, but to get there I had to walk a couple of miles along the river, then climb most of the way up the valley edge through the thick forest. In 2006 I had bivvied in the ruins of an old cottage; this time I slung my hammock from a couple of trees in the same general area. After a long flight, a long bus ride and a few miles of hiking, I was well and truly tired. The last thing I remember was the sound of a fox yipping in the woods on the other side of the valley.

My biological clock was convinced I was sleeping in, so I was completely awake, hungry and ready for action well before daybreak. I don't like to linger when I am stealth camping and was soon up, packed and mobile. There were a few puddles beside the path, one of which was completely filled with frog-spawn. This seemed like a good indicator of the overall health of the environment, although I'd noticed that the woods weren't exactly bursting with the exuberant spring bird-song I was expecting.

Part of the path intersected with a small track, strewn with branches and sawdust. Just around the corner, I came across a work crew, selectively cutting trees and saplings close to the road, who stopped work as I approached and apologised for the debris. I was a bit taken aback, but I assured them that a few fallen twigs didn't bother me much. I live in a land of massive, industrial clear-cuts, which have a far greater impact on the appearance of the landscape than a few ungathered twigs.

Monmouth is a very attractive small town with a magnificent 13th century bridge and gate house, and a monumental Catalpa tree in St. James's Square. On my earlier hike I'd walked right through the town by the shortest route and crossed the Morrow Bridge before I stopped for lunch. This time I took a longer route, ending up at the Punch House, right in the centre of town. The Punch House is a classic town pub; lots of round wooden tables, bar stools, well trodden carpet and a scattering of regulars. It was unpretentious and the food was good.

At Monmouth the Offa's Dyke path turns west, heading in the direction of the Black Mountains and Hay-on-Wye, through woods, across rolling farm fields and along short stretches of minor road. I was going nowhere near as far as Hay on Wye though. I was aiming for White Castle, and a tiny little hollow by a stream that I'd found back in 2006. It had been a longish day – about 18 miles – which may not sound like much but it was plenty for my second day.

In the morning, I shook the frost off my hammock with rapidly cooling hands and stuffed it in my pack. Sheep turned in my direction and stared as I headed up the hill back to the road, but weren't interested enough to follow me, or scared enough to run. Was I always doomed to see White Castle when there was frost on the grass and mist hanging in the ditches? As if on cue, a Barn Owl flew from the nearest tree, heading out across meadow on silent wings.

It was further from White Castle to Pandy than I remembered, across numerous fields and fences. Perhaps the beguiling view of the Black Mountains in the distance, which never seemed to get any closer, made the walk seem long, but the absence of any food or drink in my stomach may have been a major factor. I was hoping that the Lancaster

Arms in Pandy would be open, but it was closed shortly after my previous visit and was now more of a B&B.

I was really looking forward to the next part of the hike. It's a high, long ridge walk along the spine of the Black Mountains. But, I couldn't head off into the Black Mountains with no provisions and an empty stomach: I had little choice but to walk the mile to the shop in Llanvihangel Crucorney. On the way, I fell in with an older gentleman (he might have been a couple of years older than me) who was heading to the village to buy his daily newspaper and who set a cracking pace as we chatted. I dislike having to divert from my chosen route, but in his company, we covered the distance in no time.

On the way back to rejoin Offa's Dyke, my phone suddenly pinged in my pocket. Before leaving Canada I had been in touch with my old school friend John (he of Ashburton) and told him of my plans. His text indicated that he was on his way to visit friends near Presteigne. Where was I? Could we meet? So instead of heading for the hills, I took the low road towards Clodock and was soon overhauled by John in his ancient Land-rover.

Plans can change in an instant. My pack was thrown in the back with sundry ropes, pieces of wood and tools, and we headed for the pub in Clodock. It was good to sit and chat for a while. Although our lives have taken vastly different directions over the last 50 years, we have always stayed in touch – in a haphazard kind of way – and as with all really good friends, the friendship lives in the present, not buried in the shared past.

I ended up staying with John and his friends in their delightful, ancient and roomy farmhouse just outside Presteigne for the whole weekend. We walked in the nearby hills, we chatted, we visited the occasional pub. The only down side to meeting up with John was that I missed the Black Mountains altogether. It didn't make any sense to me to retrace my steps, so after saying our good-byes, I rejoined the Offa's Dyke path just north of Presteigne and continued my walk. I'd missed about 30 miles of the path.

I have come to the conclusion that isostatic rebound occurs in the Welsh border region at a pace which outstrips the post-glacial uplift in the rest of the country. How else can one account for the increased effort I had to expend to climb some of those hills? They must have grown. As a mere stripling of 55, I remember romping up the hills, barely having to pause for breath: seven years later, some of those same hills seemed interminably long and preternaturally steep.

While taking a well-earned rest after climbing the hill out of Knighton, I had the dubious pleasure of a visit from a rather impressively large male Boxer who snuffled me for a few seconds then cocked a leg and peremptorily peed on my rucksack before scooting off down hill to join his master.

Later the same day, after one long, knee jangling descent, the path passed through an enclosure filled with sheep and right past the back door of the farm house. Nobody was around, but as I left the enclosure (making sure to secure the gate behind me), I was greeted by a sheep dog who eyed me suspiciously before deciding it would be OK to grovel towards my feet. She was a lovely little thing. She could hardly get enough head scratching and petting, but seemed to live in fear of doing anything wrong. It made me a little sad to leave her,

I cursed Offa and his minions many times, during the next few miles. The earthwork and the path lead straight up one 45 degree hill, only to descend the next, time after time. Perhaps I was carrying more in my rucksack than in 2006. Perhaps I was carrying more weight in other places. Either way, the flatter lands of the Vale of Montgomery were a welcome relief.

Montgomery is a pleasant little town just to the west of Offa's Dyke. I diverted through Lymore Hall park and farm to reach the town, where I had a fine brunch in the Ivy House Café and sampled the wares of the Dragon Hotel and the Crown Inn. Of the two, the Crown was infinitely preferable; more basic, less swanky. Towards the end of the longish slog north to Welshpool, I left Offa's Dyke behind and followed the river flats into the centre of town. Although my chosen route along the tow-path of the Montgomery Canal parallels Offa's Dyke, I was now on a different leg of my journey.

In the centre of town, I went into the first pub that looked as though it might cater to locals. The few folks inside were a bit surprised to see a rucksack and rain-gear clad hiker waltz in, drop his pack, struggle out of his jacket and head for the bar. This pub satisfied me in many ways. The beer was cheap – Janner's Pride bitter from the Waen Brewery was on offer for 2 pounds a pint which seemed like an absolute bargain until I tasted it. Just kidding – it was fine! The customers at the bar eased into gentle conversation, and didn't even seem disappointed to find out that I wasn't from Kentucky or Tennessee. And when I enquired about lodgings, the bar maid rang one of her friends at a pub down the road, double checked the price (which was entirely reasonable), and booked me in. I could have stayed there at the bar for a long, long time, but I needed a shower and some supper. Pork scratchings, peanuts and crisps were just not going to be enough.

Welshpool to Whitchurch

The Westwood Park pub and B&B turned out to be ideal. It was reasonably quiet, the room was comfortable, and the breakfast in the morning was stellar and set me up for the whole day. It was too bad that I immediately started off along the canal tow-path in the wrong direction, and had to somewhat sheepishly retrace my steps before heading out of town the proper way.

Walking along the canal was dead easy, as long as I stayed attentive enough not to stray into the water or slip on some of the muddy patches. The going was soft underfoot but fortunately, rarely sloppy, and the miles just rolled by. Every so often I would come to a lock or a bridge or a long boat parked by the bank which broke the walking in to nice manageable chunks. Other than a couple of dog walkers, I had the tow-path to myself. It had become still and a little cool, and was just at the temperature where sometimes I needed my hat and sometimes I didn't, but as long as I was moving, I stayed warm.

Stretches of the canal have long been abandoned and were overgrown with reeds or even so choked that there was no longer any sign of water – just a broad, shallow scoop next to the path. In others, the process of rehabilitation was well under-way with large machines working to re-excavate and re-line the canal bed to bring it back in to action. Once the whole thing is navigable again, boats will come, bringing new trade to a rather overlooked part of the country.

I left the canal briefly and wandered in to Llanymynech looking for something for lunch. Despite looking more like an Edwardian private house than a pub, the Bradford Arms was open and offered food, so I ventured in. While I nursed my first pint and awaited a pie and chips, the burly gentleman at the next table engaged me in conversation. He had no trouble at all immediately pegging me as a Canadian, as he'd spent much of his career as the principal of a school in Newfoundland and had travelled extensively in the rest of Canada. Newfoundlanders, of course speak English in their own charming and incomprehensible way, but if he'd picked up anything of a Newfoundland accent, it was now deeply buried in the Welsh.

For the first half of the day, there had been low hills on the west side of the canal. From Llanymynech on, the canal cut through much flatter and lower scenery as it headed towards its junction with the Llangollen canal. It was actually quite a nice change to be walking surrounded by well cultivated crop fields; I'd left the sheep pastures behind.

I scuttled across the busy A5 between Oswestry and Shrewsbury and headed straight in to the Queen's Head, right next to the canal.

Presumably it once catered to the canal trade, and, from the outside, has that attractive 19th century canal architecture look about it, but it felt like a road house to me and I didn't stay long.

Evening was fast approaching. It was still late February and the days were short. This section of the canal is raised above the surrounding terrain, so I had extensive views across the floodplain of the River Perry. The sun was low on the horizon and about to disappear. I was beginning to wonder whether I would actually find a sufficiently secluded spot to sling my hammock when I came across a small break in the vegetation with just enough space for me to attach my ropes to the surrounding thorn bushes. It wasn't as well hidden as I would have liked, but as it was unlikely that too many people would be along that remote part of the tow-path at that time of the evening, it would do.

It was going to be cold. I filled the insulating pockets which hang beneath the hammock with my spare clothes, tucked my camper matt beneath my double sleeping bags, quickly stripped naked, pulled on my thermal underwear and polar fleece hat and clambered in. I spent a little time writing some notes on my phone and looking at the day's photographs before going to sleep. If it was as late as 7.30, I'd be surprised.

Long nights, cold weather and a beer supper are a poor mix where bladders are concerned. At about 1AM, I left my comfortable nest and braved the chilly night air. It was worth it. The sky was remarkably clear, there was little light pollution and the stars were visible in large numbers, but since my bare feet were melting the frost, I jumped back in as soon as I could.

There was a thick frost covering everything when I woke up, and the canal was frozen solid. As you can imagine, I didn't linger over getting dressed, packed and ready to walk again, stopping only to see if I could break the ice with my fist (I couldn't). The sun was still below the horizon, casting a faint yellow glow in the tops of the bushes. All was quiet, except for the occasional cawing of a crow in the distance. I love mornings like this; they are well worth any slight discomfort they bring.

I soon warmed up as I started walking, and in no time was at the junction of the two canals. The day was warming fast too. By the time I reached Ellesmere the frost was gone and all that was left of the ice was a thin skim in the shadows. The canal skirts the village of Ellesmere, but passes close to one of the 'meres' for which the area is famous. These are ponds which formed when large blocks of glacial ice melted, leaving depressions which eventually filled with water. Although quite small (the largest 'The Mere' being about 48 Ha.) they are carefully managed and rather attractive. The one I was passing - Blake Mere -was surrounded by trees, and at this time of the morning, and this time of year, was remarkably tranquil.

I was still enjoying my canal-side walk. By holding a contour, canals wind through the countryside in unusual ways and are cross-grained to the rest of the countryside. Being relatively modern (in British terms, of course) they interrupt field boundaries, cross roads at odd angles and give a unique view of the world.

A few miles east of Ellesmere the Llangollen canal passed along the side of the vast, waterlogged, open area of Fenn's Moss, or more accurately, The Fenn's, Whixall, Bettisfield, Wem & Cadney Moss Complex. At 948 hectares (2340 acres) this is Britain's third largest lowland raised bog. Much of the area used to be cut for peat, but this has stopped now and nature is being allowed (or is being helped) to return the bogs to their natural state. From the canal, it looks like a broad, slightly hummocky green – brown......bog, which of course, it is.

I had to chuckle at the 'For your safety' warning on the information board, which cautioned you to 'Watch out for adders; if bitten, keep calm and seek medical attention'. Gosh, I didn't realise that adders were such a risk to health and safety, and that by entering the area, you were taking your life in your hands. The reality is that adders are unlikely to launch themselves at you from every burrow or bank and that if you get bitten, it almost certainly because you've been daft enough to pick one up. They are uncommon and highly unlikely to be much of a problem. Still, I suppose the warning adds a little spice and sense of adventure to a soggy walk across the Moss.

My own walk was far from soggy. The tow path was nicely soft underfoot. Most of the time I was walking on short grass – very easy on the legs and feet. Usually I'm fairly tired by the end of the day, but when I reached Whitchurch I still had plenty of energy.

Whitchurch is a nice little town, with plenty of half-timber buildings and a thriving main shopping street. My Norfolk friend Andrew had grown up here, so I set myself the task of trying to guess which pubs he'd frequented. Like me, Andrew has a taste for the genuine and the earthy, so I hunted around for any pubs that looked as though they hadn't been messed with too much. The Old Eagles on Watergate seemed like just the place. It occupies a nondescript building with a painted brick front, sandwiched between a sporting goods store and a rather tired looking private dwelling. The inside was basic and didn't look as though it had changed much in the last thirty years. The men at the bar looked as though they had just dropped in for a pint or two after work, before heading home for supper. My arrival sparked barely any interest – just a nod of acknowledgement. I was left to drop my pack, get a drink and find a seat in peace. My B&B was just down the road, so I was in no great hurry to leave.

Whitchurch to Matlock to Miller's Dale

My original plan had been to hike between Whitchurch and the southern end of the Pennines on the South Cheshire Way but by the time I had walked for four hours out of Whitchurch, I'd had enough. The scenery was acceptable – a pleasant mix of farms, farm land and pasture – but to me it felt crowded and busy. Everywhere I looked I could see brick bungalows and houses, rooftops, church steeples and roads. At lunch time I headed across the fields to the Bhurtpore Inn in Aston. I was early, so I sat outside making a few notes until the bar tender kindly invited me to sit inside until they opened. It was warm and comfortable in the Bhurtpore, as I sat, trying to decide how to proceed. The idea of walking though such a fully settled landscape had no appeal for me, and I was having a hard time visualizing how I would find a place to rest my head once evening came. After sampling two or three of the beers they had on offer, as the weekend was fast approaching, I decided to back-track to the railway station at Wrenbury, take the train to Crewe then drop down for the obligatory visit to my brother and his wife in Birmingham.

Two days later I was heading north again on a train to Matlock in Derbyshire. I'd spent a couple of years as a student there, living in the main town and in the village of Bonsall, walking the surrounding hills whenever I didn't feel like going to class – which was often. Once again, I'd eaten a big chunk out of my original plan, but rather than feeling regretful, I was looking forward to stretching my legs on the high limestone plateaus of the Derbyshire Dales and the southern Peak District.

The sign for the Limestone Way was a mere stone's throw from the railway station, so within minutes, I had left Matlock behind and was struggling up the steep hill to the west of the town. When I lived in Bonsall, this was my regular walk home over the hills, and it was pleasant to see how little it had changed in 43 years, although I think the hill might have become a little steeper. After about a mile, I noticed a Land Rover parked in one of the fields and a couple of men walking either side of a dry stone wall with shotguns. I stopped briefly, then started walking again, once I was sure that they had seen me. They were after rabbits, perhaps on their own land, but I had a perfect right to be walking on the public footpath and a couple of guys with .410s weren't about to dissuade me.

As I got within talking distance of one of the hunters, a rabbit suddenly broke cover and raced across the field. It didn't get far. A shot rang out and he tumbled, kicking in the grass. The hunters seemed a little surprised to watch me calmly walking on after congratulating them on their shot. If they were expecting me to be intimidated, or distressed in a tree-huggery way, they were disappointed.

It was only four miles from Matlock to Winster, but after stopping briefly to take a picture of the delightful 18th century Winster Market House and buy a few supplies in the village shop, I ambled through the village, past stone cottages and along stone wall lined roads to the Miner's Standard pub. I'd been on the move since early morning and a little liquid refreshment seemed in order.

I was being really lucky with the weather. Even though it was still only early March, the skies were clear and hazily blue-grey and I was able to walk quite comfortably just in a t-shirt and polar fleece over-shirt. Now that I look at the map, the area seems to have just as many buildings and roads as the terrain near Crewe, but it felt much more open and remote. I suppose reality has little to do with how one feels about a place; the stone walls, sheep pastures, stunted oaks and hawthorns in the hedgerows and the unexpected valleys which only revealed themselves once you were virtually on top of them, appealed to me.

As I lingered to take in the view of the Bradford River valley above Youlgreave I watch an elderly man making his way up. He must have been well into his eighties, tall, with a fine posture and while he wasn't moving fast, he covered ground steadily. As he approached, he eyed my pack and we slipped effortlessly into conversation about hiking, camping and travelling. I got the impression that here was a high-powered man who had done noteworthy and adventurous things in his life, who still derived a huge amount of pleasure walking up a small hill close to his home. I hope I still have plenty of vitality at his age.

The Limestone Way skirts Youlgreave and so did I, choosing to follow the path along the stream for a mile or so, before climbing up the side of the valley and across rolling sheep pasture towards Monyash. I though briefly about finding somewhere to stay in, or near Monyash, but it was still too early in the day and I wasn't really ready to stop. Once again, the paths were quiet and I was able to ramble along, lost in my own thoughts.

At times like this my thoughts sometimes stray to wondering whether I would like to return to Britain to live, and if so, where and why. I'm fond of Norfolk, I like the Pennines, the border counties near Wales are nice – but always, my thinking returns to practical concerns.

How would I live? What kind of house could we afford (something dingy and tiny – British house prices are outrageous)? Could I tolerate the summer crowds and busy roads? The answer is no!

Many emigrants return to the UK to retire to the chocolate box cottage of their dreams. I wonder whether it works out well for them. I hope it does. No matter how attractive an idea it might seem, it is not on my horizon. In a world of Aesop's 'Ants and Grasshoppers', I've always been a grasshopper, using up whatever resources I had at my disposal, ill preparing myself for the winter of life. Fortunately, I have no interest in returning permanently, even if I had the wherewithal. The idea of living out my golden years in that metaphorical cottage is fundamentally unappealing. I'm not ready to be old.

With these happy thoughts, I upped my pace along the narrow wall-lined road through Flagg, heading in the general direction of Miller's Dale. The light was fading fast - this happened every day, and every day I was never ready for it - so I started to look for a suitable place to rest my head before it got too dark. From the farm track I was following, I could see car lights on the Buxton – Bakewell Road in the distance. I stopped at the first flattish square of grass at the side of the road and spent a while sitting on a wall eating a Mars Bar while I decided whether to pitch my hammock as a bivvy.

By the time I had made up my mind to carry on a bit further, it was completely dark and time to dig my head lamp out of my pack. This was turning out to have been a long day. Since getting off the train in Matlock I'd walked at least 16 miles. I wasn't too tired, but I was starting to get hungry, and as usual, didn't have much worth eating in my pack.

I checked the map. Miller's Dale wasn't more than a couple of miles away and the OS map showed a PH (pub) in the village. Oh well, it was worth a look: I'd work out 'plan B' if I had to, once I got there.

Miraculously the pub was open and serving meals. As I was the only customer, I had a long chat with the bar maid about her photography career aspirations. She reminded me of my daughter; smart, articulate and thoughtful – and best of all, she didn't mind chatting to an old grey haired hiker who, for once, was happy to sit, drink, talk, drink, eat, drink and talk some more.

I could feel the beer starting to have an effect, and I knew the shuffle-board crowd would be arriving soon to fill the place up, so I took my leave and headed out into the night. The map showed a Youth Hostel about a mile along the valley, so I switched on my light and headed that way, only to find it was closed. I retraced my steps back to the village, jumped a wall and found a nice little patch of grass sandwiched between the wall and the river. There was no way to hang my hammock, so I just laid it out on the ground, got in my sleeping bag and was soon (I suspect) startling the local wildlife with my snoring.

Miller's Dale to Crowden

It was still completely dark when I awoke but I was eager to get moving; the idea of having to explain what I was doing there did not appeal to me. For all I knew, I might have been sleeping in someone's back garden.

Once again, there had been a stiff frost. The chill in the air helped me pack quickly and before long I was heading north along the narrow track which ultimately led to Castleton. There was old, hard snow in the gully between the walls, frost on the fields, mist in the valleys and, as the light emerged from the east, the beginnings of a blue sky. It was going to be a glorious day.

This was familiar country from my caving days while at college in Matlock. The well known and publicly accessible (for a fee) caves near Castleton, such as Blue John, Speedwell and Peak Cavern are a fraction of the innumerable pot holes which dot the region. Less well know but more testing pot holes such as Giants Hole, Eldon Hole and P8 lead to extensive networks of underground halls, tunnels and stream channels which require proper equipment, experience and training to explore safely.

The Limestone Way follows an old glacial valley, made deeper when the roof of subterranean stream channels collapsed, deepening the already impressive divot in the landscape. It makes for an impressive and scenic entrance to the village, passing directly below the walls of Peveril Castle.

It was still fairly early in the morning, so I looked around for somewhere to get some breakfast, ending up in the Old Nag's Head, right in the heart of the village. There were enough 'come-along' signs on the outside walls to make me think it was a touristy place where everything would be over-priced and of marginal quality, but I needn't have worried. The 'Award Winning Derbyshire Breakfast' was fine and my wallet emerged only slightly thinner than before. Besides, I liked the part of the sign that said 'Kids, Dogs, Muddy Boots, Everyone Welcome'. My, how times have changed! I once saw a sign outside an English pub saying 'No Dogs or Children Allowed!'

The high ridge between Castleton and the Vale of Edale is the southernmost edge of the 'Dark Peak' – the part of the Pennines formed of Shales and Sandstones, as opposed to the limestone of the lands to the south through which I'd just been walking. The change in scenery was almost immediate. Instead of the high, relatively flat table-lands of the southern Pennines, where dry stone walls line every field and sheep graze on rich green pasture, the Dark Peak was all steep slopes, tussocky grass, with knots of woodland on the lower slopes.

With my heavy pack, the path up to the crest of the ridge below Back Tor had my heart racing and me sweating and stripped down to my t-shirt. I was happy to spend a little time fussing with my cameras at the top to give my heart a chance to find a more normal beat. Across the valley, I could just see the bulky mass of Kinder Scout emerging through the haze while to the right, the steep cliff of Back Tor seemed only an arms reach away.

As I was on the last few hundred yards of the slope, I'd noticed a figure working his way along the ridge from the direction of the Mam Tor hill fort, about a mile to the west. Bill - let's call him Bill - was moving slowly and was a little bent, but was making steady progress. By the time I was finished with the cameras and just about to hoist my pack, he arrived at the intersection of the paths.

We exchanged the normal pleasantries about the weather, and as soon as he heard my voice and noticed my pack, the conversation inevitably started around where I was from and where I was going. Bill said he was a little envious as he didn't think he'd be able to do anything quite that strenuous – he'd had open heart surgery just six weeks before.

I was the only person in the Edale youth hostel that night. The bathrooms had recently been renovated to provide easy access for people with disabilities. I had a luxurious shower in a room big enough to soak a dozen people (or manhandle a wheelchair), before heading downstairs for supper, cooked just for me, by the cook. People pay big money for this kind of luxury.

The youth hostel's WiFi allowed me to be in email contact with my wife back at home. Shortly before I had left, my father-in-law had been diagnosed with terminal cancer so I felt a real need to be in fairly constant contact. Chris was handling the situation with her normal strength and common sense, but I was starting to feel awkward about being away from the family when perhaps I was needed at home. She assured me that everything was under control, but I still couldn't banish the thought that it was an difficult and unreasonable time for me to be away. After 33 years of marriage, I'd known Chris's father longer than I had known my own - my father had died when I was 24 – In retrospect, I can see that the news of his illness had hit me harder than I realised.

These thoughts were churning in the back of my mind as I made my way up the steep and rugged Grindsbrook path towards the edge of the Kinder Scout plateau. As I climbed higher up the valley, the mist descended, obscuring all but a few feet in any direction. I was using the GPS on my phone in conjunction with 1:50,000 scale digital 'Memory Maps' to guide me, but in the thick mist, I soon lost the path across to the waterfall at Kinder Downfall and started to follow a sheep path. The top of Kinder Scout is a boggy, hummocky maze of erosion channels, each indistinguishable from the next – especially in the fog, and I was soon turned around and unsure of the direction I should be heading. Once I realised my mistake, I tried to rely on the GPS signal on the map to guide me in the right direction but I could see my track on the map was starting to become a confused zig-zag line, not heading anywhere useful. I knew I couldn't be too far from the proper path, but no matter how many attempts I made, I just couldn't find it.

It was actually rather amusing to find myself lost. This was something that happened to other people, not experienced hikers like me. I'd been over Kinder Scout many times. How could I have got myself into this dilemma?

I stopped aimlessly walking, sat on my pack and had a quick snack while I thought about it. What I needed was a clear direction to follow. Of course, my compass! I reached into my pack and pulled out my old Silva. Using the compass needle to orient the digital map, I set a bearing for Kinder Downfall. It took less than five minutes following that bearing before I regained the proper path. I kept checking the bearing to make sure I wasn't being led astray by yet another sheep path, but before long at was at the waterfall and completely back on track. Sometimes, old technology is the best!

The rest of the day was a steady slog in the mist across Kinder Scout and Bleaklow. I met no-one. It was eerily quiet, with no wind, no bird calls, just the sound of my feet slapping in the little puddles caught in the rough surface of the paving slabs and the rhythmic creak of my pack. And it was oddly disorientating. With no landmarks to show the passage of distance, each step looked like the previous one. It was if I was walking in place.

Since our time hiking together on the Pennine Way, John and I had been in regular email contact. When I my son Alex was in the UK, John had met him at Halifax bus station and had been an exemplary host and tour guide for a few days. They even climbed Black Hill together, so John could show him where we first met.

As I made my way down Clough Edge towards the Torside Reservoir in Longdendale I thought, perhaps John would like to join me for a little while, so I gave him a call. We arranged to meet at the

Crowden Youth Hostel. I still had a couple of miles to walk: he had about 40 miles to drive.

Hiking with John again

I'd had plenty of time to chill off by the time John arrived and was happy to be sitting in his warm car as we headed off to Halifax. On the way to his home, I got him to stop at a shop so I could at least arrive with some sort of offering. He and his wife Norma were going to be feeding and housing me for the night – the least I could do was to grab a bottle of wine.

In the shop, the young guy behind the counter asked me where I was from, and hearing Canada, said something that struck me as odd and perhaps a little sad.

"Are Asian people welcome in Canada?"

I said that they were. Canada is a land of immigrants (First Nations people excepted). There are people there from all over the world, especially in the cities and as far as I could tell, there was less of a tendency for people to congregate in cultural ghettos than I had noticed in the UK.

"Of course" I added, "there are ignorant and racist people everywhere".

In the back of my mind I was already thinking about cutting my hike short and returning to Canada early, so I was quite pleased when John started talking about going straight to the Lake District the next day. This would mean I would, once again, be carving a huge chunk out of my original plan, and I would miss re-visiting a long stretch of the Pennine Way, but as I've said before, plans can change in an instant.

In the morning we loaded up John's car and were soon on the M6 heading towards Penrith, Keswick and a camp-site John frequently used in Braithwaite.

Having spent the last few decades free camping in the Canadian Bush, or, more occasionally staying in Provincial Parks, where each site has it's own fire pit, picnic table and manicured (usually gravel) camping area designed for an RV or caravan, English camp-sites seem strange. The one at Braithwaite was at the luxury end of the scale. The camping area was as flat as a soccer field and about the same size. The shower and toilets building was custom built and sparklingly clean. Others I had seen were little more than a muddy field with a tap and a toilet.

We pitched our tent between the main office and the toilets – well away from most of the other campers, but close enough to the facilities for my inevitable night-time wanderings. It was quiet and pleasant, but it still felt as though I was camping in the middle of town, even if there were mountains all around.

In the morning, John led the way up the long steady climb to the top of Grasmoor. It was cold and windy, but since the air was clear, we enjoyed excellent views across to some of the higher peaks, where little strips of snow could be seen lying in the hollows. My heart wasn't really in it though, and I was just as happy to head back down to the village for a couple of pints in the Royal Oak.

John tried his best to talk me in to climbing Skiddaw the following morning, but I was feeling lazy and without the spirit for a long, tough climb, especially since we could see that snow and strong winds were already blowing over the top of the mountain. Instead, we opted for a rather less strenuous circumnavigation of Derwent Water; a peaceful gentle walk paralleling the lake shore. A very pleasant walk it was too. As usual, we kept up a constant chatter about hiking, mountains, adventures and family while the miles rolled easily beneath our feet. At Castle Crag we clambered over the loose debris from quarrying to the flat terrace at the war memorial and had a bite to eat while we enjoyed the views stretching in all directions. Just as we were about to leave, three hikers joined us, each of whom must have been well in to their seventies – if not more.

I know how I felt after the climb up to the summit. I had been breathing hard and was quite happy when the top came into view. These three arrived looking fresh, as if clambering up tricky, precipitous mountain sides was an everyday thing. Perhaps, for them, it was.

They graciously allowed me to take their picture before we left them to eat their lunch in peace while we descended to Borrowdale. I'm still in admiration; great people. They were a perfect illustration of the value of regular fresh air and exercise; I doubt I'd seen a single hiker under thirty since leaving Chepstow.

After a short morning hike in the woods above Braithwaite, we packed up and headed back to Halifax. I suspect this was a bit of a disappointment for John, but I was finding myself increasingly unsettled and distracted. Back in Halifax, I was able to book an early flight back to Canada, leaving me just a couple of days to zip over to Norfolk to spend the weekend with Andrew and Julia before catching the train to London and the flight home.

On most of my trips I have usually been able to stick, more-or-less to my original plan. This time, however, it all fell apart. Chris's father died later the same year.

Actually, I'm English

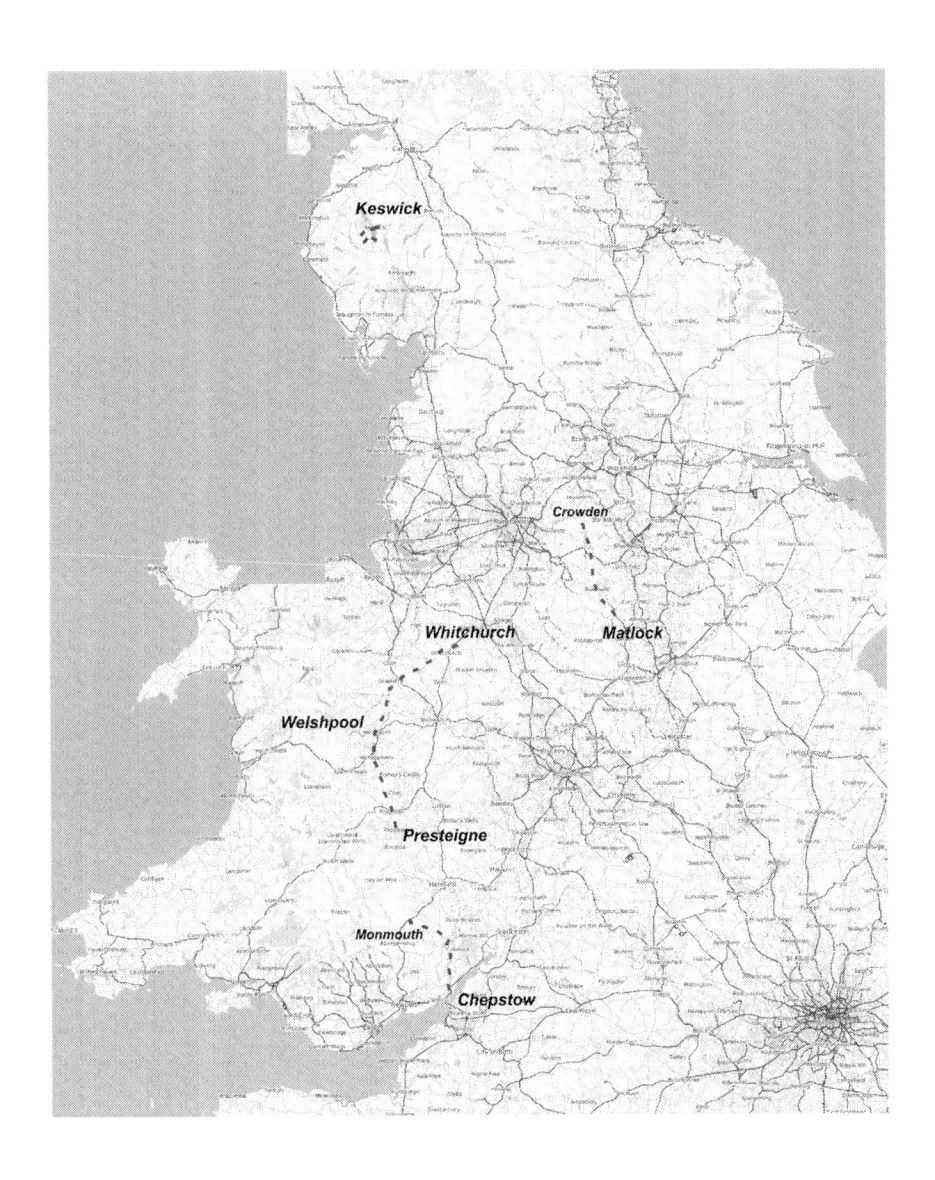

Chepstow Castle

Offa's Dyke: still quite an impressive scar on the landscape

Early morning on the Montgomery Canal

Early morning heading towards Castleton

John above Derwent Water

PART 5

COAST TO COAST
- CLOUGHTON TO ST. BEES -

Planes, trains and buses

It's the dead of winter and after dark. Snow banks three feet high line the roads. No tarmac is visible, just hard packed ice and snow. A single figure carrying a full rucksack passes by, his headlamp beam illuminating the snow as he treads the lonely road. His balaclava has just a narrow slit for his eyes, which squint through the driving snow. He walks by purposefully, mindful of the treacherous footing and disappears into the night.

Such a sight would have seemed a bit strange, if there had been anyone to see, but my neighbours were all inside, staying warm in front of the TV while I was out trudging the streets. This was my nightly preparation as I struggled to get my body ready for another long walk, and put some miles on my new boots.

The winter of 2014 was a long one in Ontario (I have a feeling I may have said something like this before...). It dragged on endlessly and I got lazy and dispirited. My motorbikes stayed untouched in the garage; it was too cold to go out and tinker, and anyway I couldn't summon the enthusiasm. The reports I was preparing on the previous season's field work were well in hand, but I was finding it increasingly hard to drag myself down to my office each day. I needed a change of scenery, a mid winter break, an expedition, something to shake me out of my torpor.

But where and what? Pennine Way – done it. Wales – been there three times in the last few years. I thought long and hard about the

Southern Upland Way in Scotland, even going so far as to download all the necessary topographical maps, but the logistics of getting from Canada to Port Patrick to start wouldn't fall easily in to place, no matter how much time I spent on the Internet, looking at flight destinations, bus routes and train schedules.

In the end, the only long distance hiking trail that really appealed to me which was easily accessible was the Coast-to-Coast Walk – a 192 mile transect across northern England from the North Sea on the Yorkshire Moors coast to the Irish Sea, west of the Lake District. The walk had first been brought to public attention by Arthur Wainwright in his 1973 book *'A Coast to Coast Walk'* which provided route suggestions – the expectation being that you would devise your own route based on the overall conception. This appealed to me.

I knew the Coast-to-Coast had become quite popular in the last few years, with numerous companies offering guided trips, baggage hauling and easy overnight stops, but after my experience on the Pennine Way, I doubted whether it would be crowded in late February and early March. Most people are far too sensible to be stalking across the hills when the wind is up, the snow is falling and the nights are cool.

Traditionally, the Coast-to-Coast is walked from west to east, so the prevailing wind is always behind you. Assuming I knew better than Wainwright and everyone else, I opted to hike from east to west, leaving the more precipitous terrain of the Lake District until the last parts of the hike. I was hoping that by then I would have shed a few pounds and gained a bit of fitness and strength, sorely lacking after a months of inactivity.

Starting in the east also made the most logistical sense for me. As usual, the trans-Atlantic flight from Toronto to Manchester was something to be endured. For once though, the atmospheric winds were with us and we made record time, touching down well ahead of schedule. Baggage retrieval and customs went equally smoothly. I was able to head for the railway platform and the train to Manchester Piccadilly well ahead of my expectations.

I have ridden the train between Manchester Airport and down-town Manchester numerous times and it never ceases to amaze me. Throughout the whole journey, I don't think I saw a single fragment of ground that hadn't been built on, paved, concreted, demolished or turned into some kind of disgusting wasteland. Oh there was some green stuff: dissolute looking weeds growing between cracks in old factory floors, postage stamp lawns in grim suburbs, shrubs and trees growing out of the railway embankments between broken shopping carts, bicycle frames and other backyard spillage. It is not the most prepossessing entrance to

Beautiful Britain.

I had a bit of time to kill before my pre-booked, and remarkably cheap train to Scarborough, so I spent my time searching for a pay-as-you-go phone card and cruising for industrial sausage rolls. The latter were easy to find and as bizarrely satisfying as ever. The former, however, proved more of a problem. After no luck at a number of outlets, I eventually found some cards on a store display. When I queried the counter clerk whether this would allow me to access phone and data service, I was assured that it was exactly what I was looking for. It wasn't! When I loaded the card and tried to connect to the service provider, they refused my credit card. Apparently, you need a UK credit card not one from a banana republic like Canada. How incredibly insular and daft is that? OK rant over – for now.

The train ride to Scarborough was pleasant enough, cutting a diagonal swath across the Pennines and the Vale of York before disgorging me at the Scarborough station. I'd spent quite a bit of time looking at Google Streetview before setting off; enough to convince me that I wanted nothing to do with starting my walk from the station, since it would oblige me to traverse miles of urban streets before I hit the coast. Instead, I jumped on a local bus heading north towards Whitby, which dropped me off in the village of Cloughton.

Wainwright's route starts in Robin Hood's Bay then follows a rather erratic route to the Esk Valley and Glaisdale. My plan was to follow the Cleveland Way along the coast from Cloughton to Ravenscar, then turn inland, following a straight path almost due west across the North York Moors, meeting up with the 'official' route a couple of miles before the Lion Inn at Farndale.

It was less than a mile along a narrow lane from where the bus left me to the sea cliffs at Cloughton Wyke, with fields on either side and the smell of the sea in the air. I was still in my travelling clothes, so I stopped at the bench at the end of the road, changed in to my hiking gear, adjusted my pack, had a quick snack, then headed north along the Cleveland Way, which hugs the top of the cliff like a limpet. The path was a green ribbon between a wire fence and the edge of England, which at this point was an almost vertical drop to the rocks 300 feet below. The weather was clear and calm, with only a slight breeze. Far off in the distance, a large ship was slowly making it's way up the coast, seemingly keeping pace with me. Although I was tired, the cool air and quiet were invigorating, the walking was easy and I was full of 'first day' enthusiasm.

It had taken me most of the day to get from Manchester Airport to the start of the hike and even before I started walking, long shadows were fingering their way across the fields. I thought briefly about where I would stay, noticing a few nice spots on the top of the cliff which would suit my little bivvy perfectly, but it was still too early to stop and I wanted to get some miles behind me. As I had hoped, I had the cliff tops almost completely to myself. I did pass one woman walking her dog, but when I said hello, she gave me a suspicious look and scurried past. We were on Beast Cliff – perhaps that had made her anxious.

A little further along I turned inland along a single track road heading towards Ravenscar. I wondered whether there would be a pub or B&B, but soon banished those thoughts; it was going to be a nice night – what better than a night on the moors?

My map showed a nice straight path cutting directly across Fylingdales Moor from a radio mast just west of Ravenscar. It seemed the most logical and direct path across the moors. What I hadn't realised at the time was that by chance, I had chosen the route of the Lyke Wake Walk – a 40 mile challenge walk, ending near Osmotherley.

For now though, I was just interested in sleep. By the time I got to the radio mast it was almost dark. I headed down the well worn track for a few hundred yards, found a flattish area of heather, rolled out my bivvy sack and sleeping bag, made a haphazard shelter with my tarp and hiking poles and promptly fell asleep.

Stalked across the Moors?

Three hours later I was wide awake. My body was telling me it was morning and time to get up and get moving; my watch told me it was 9PM. It had started to drizzle. I couldn't just lie there, wide awake, for another 10 hours until sunrise, so I quickly packed my gear, dug out my head lamp and headed out across the moor.

You might think that hiking across the North York Moors in the dark in the rain was a bit daft, pointless or perhaps even dangerous, but actually it was really rather magical. Away from major sources of light pollution, night time visibility can be surprisingly good. I could see the general shape of the moorland all around me, it's edge punctuated by numerous pinpoints of light from farmhouses and street lights, while my head lamp illuminated the path ahead.

After an hour or two of steady walking, I stopped for a quick snack and a chance to savour the night. All was quiet and calm, the broad flat shape of the moors now visible whichever direction I turned. Looking back along my path, I could still see some specks of light from Ravenscar, one of which caught my attention as it seemed to be moving, flickering, and gaining and losing intensity. I stood for a long time looking at that light but since I couldn't make any sense of it, started walking again.

Every so often I would stop for a few moments. Yes, the light was still there and it still seemed to be moving. Was this some trick of distance, light and atmospheric moisture, or was someone actually following me? Who else would be crazy enough to be walking across the North York Moors in the middle of the night by the light a of head lamp? I stopped to look again. Yes, the light was still flickering. I could only think of one (other) person daft enough.

While I was back in Canada I had been in touch with John – the hiker I had originally met on Black Hill during my Pennine Way walk. By an amazing coincidence, he was going to be leading a hiking group on the moors a few days ahead of my arrival in Scarborough. Once he was done with them, he was going to return home briefly, then catch the train to Kirkby Stephen so we could walk the second half of the Coast-to-Coast together.

I constructed the theory that John found out my train time, looked at the map, figured out my plan and decided to follow me. I thought of waiting but I was still unsure whether the light truly was moving or whether the distance and air moisture were playing tricks on me. The gradually increasing tempo of the rain encouraged me to walk on. If it was John, he'd be able to follow my tracks easily enough in the soggy ground and knowing the speed he travelled, he'd soon catch up. If it wasn't him, then there was no point in hanging around.

In some places the path was a narrow gravel road, in others, little more than a well trodden soggy divot in the surface of the moor. My head lamp illuminated enough of the path ahead for me to be sure of the direction I needed to travel. From time to time, I would look at the Memory-Map Ap on my phone and the little red ring showing my GPS location confirmed that I was still on track.

Hours passed, the intensity of the rain increased and the ground became puddle strewn and soggy. Passing near the fence above RAF Fylingdale I wondered whether my middle-of-the-night passage was being monitored by video or motion sensors, but if it was, nobody was sufficiently interested to brave the wet weather to check me out. My unsynchronized circadian rhythms were also letting me know that it was time for a proper sleep this time. I found a section of fence where the Goathland Road meets the A169. Strung up my tarp, rolled out my bivvy bag and fell to sleep to the sound of the rain pattering down.

On to Osmotherley

The sun was up and shining strongly when I awoke. There was no sign of the previous night's rain and not a cloud in the sky. Since there was also no sign of John, the light I had been monitoring must have been a figment of my imagination, but I wouldn't have been the least bit surprised to have seen his tent parked next to my bivvy.

It didn't take long for me to pack my gear and hit the trail again. The path led virtually due west, the route punctuated by a series of standing stones, cists and cairns. Before I had left Canada, I had read that a brush fire had burned the moor over a broad area, unexpectedly exposing a preserved prehistoric landscape, but where I was walking, only the most obvious monuments were visible through the heather and bracken.

Before long, I had crossed Howl Moor (don't you just love these names?), descended into a valley, negotiated the stepping stones at Wheeldale Beck, climbed the steep valley side over the old Roman Road and headed across Wheeldale Moor. It was a world of muted colours and hazy skies; the lower slopes of the brown moor abruptly changing to areas of yellowish green on the lower slopes, with dark green plantations clogging some of the valleys. With no high hills, precipices or crags, the moors are not a dramatic landscape, but they feel high, wild and remote. I had yet to see another hiker.

Although they only protrude a few feet out of the surface of the moor, the ancient standing stones and cairns act as effective way markers. I suspect that has been part of their function for a very long time, helping travellers find their way across an otherwise virtually featureless plateau. I stopped briefly at the *'Blue Man-i'-th'-Moss'* one of the more prominent stones, for a drink of water. It looked more like the termite nests you might see on the African Savannah than a Neolithic rock, but it did its job well and was visible from hundreds of yards away. For the most part, the walking was easy, many feet having worn a narrow path through the heather and peat to the rock and gravel below. A few lower sections were boggy though, and I managed to accidentally explore one of those with my boot, sinking up to my knee before I was able to extricate myself.

Eventually my path intersected with the small road skirting the rim of the River Seven valley, and ultimately led to the Lion Inn at Farndale, my destination – if they had room for me – for the night.

I had expected to pay through the nose to stay at the Lion, so was pleasantly surprised to be shown to comfortable room which only required sacrificing a few unnecessary body parts. After laying out my wet gear to dry, downing a couple of pints of Theakstons, eating a rather good hamburger supper and watching a little TV, I was ready for bed.

I could barely see across the Lion's parking lot as I put my boots and gaiters on in the morning. A thick mist had descended during the night, soaking everything and turning the world grey. By the time I was ready to leave, the cloud base had risen to just above the moor and it had started to rain. Oh well – at least I should be able to see where I was going, even at the price of getting wet.

The first few miles of this day's walk promised to be an easy stroll along the bed of an abandoned railway which once transported iron ore from nearby mines, but which now provides flat walking for five miles around the head of the Farndale Valley. It turned out to be a bit of a slog through driving rain and strong head winds for the first couple of hours until the clouds lifted, the rain stopped and the wind dropped. For most of the rest of the day, my route once again joined the Cleveland Way – a long distance path which I had once foolishly discounted as uninteresting, but which I now found to be excellent walking. This section of the path follows the edge of the Cleveland Hills, providing quiet, ridge top walking and extensive views across the flat fertile lands of the Vale Of York all the way north to Middlesborough. I was a bit shocked to be able to see the sea about 12 miles away - surely I'd walked more than that in the past two days - but when I looked at a broader scale map, I could see that the coast swung around to the north-west, so I didn't feel quite so bad.

Where the Cleveland Way crosses the 'B' road north to Stokesley I sat on a bit of broken wall, took off my boots and socks and had some cheese and crackers for lunch. It was barely lunch time, but I was feeling a bit flat and in serious need of something to perk me up. The idea of heading straight up the steep bank across the road didn't strike me as any fun at all, so I cheated and took the low road along the north edge of the Broughton Plantation. This avoided climbing up to two high points along the ridge, but meant that I had to pick my way through innumerable muddy puddles in order to hug the contour. I couldn't avoid all climbs though and was soon clambering back to a high outlook with an astonishingly clear view across the plain. I was happy to see the distinctive shape of Roseberry Topping about 7 miles away to the north-east above Great Ayton.

Back when our children were young, Christine and I had climbed that hill - or to put it more accurately, Chris had climbed it, Sam had bounced up it, Emily had dragged herself moaning and complaining (we subsequently found out she had Fifth disease so had a good excuse) while I carried Alex - the youngest, but by no means the lightest! I think that day is firmly etched in all our memories.

By mid afternoon the weather had changed completely. Soft billowy clouds dotted the sky and the air was clear and pleasantly cool. I had regained some energy too, striding along the Cleveland Way with plenty of vigour and enthusiasm. Parts of the Cleveland Way have been slabbed but I was used to them from hiking the Pennine Way and found them neither intrusive nor difficult to walk on. Eventually the path left the upper ridge and dropped down to lower ground through heavily wooded slopes before meeting the road at Scarth. Once again I had decided a comfortable bed and a pint was in order. I took the paved road past Cod Beck Reservoir to Osmotherley.

I immediately liked Osmotherley. It seemed an unpretentious place of robust stone houses, pan tile roofs and broad, well maintained greens. The first pub I came to quoted me an ambitious price for bed and breakfast, but just at that moment, I didn't care and happily handed over my credit card. After a quick wash and change of foot ware, I sampled the other two pubs in the village, concluding that sometimes first choices are the best. When I returned, the young man behind the bar showed more than a polite interest in my travels. As we talked, it became clear that he was dithering about whether to concentrate on his career or go off travelling. - something he'd dreamed of for a long time. We talked about the pros and cons and I tried not to influence his decision too much with my own opinions, but when I left for bed, I couldn't refrain from telling him what my motorcycling friend Norm often says: "You spend a long time dead!"

A Change of Plan

Earlier in the evening I had chatted briefly with some hikers who were also staying at the pub, and we resumed our conversation over breakfast. They had walked the Coast-to-Coast a few years back and when they heard I was meeting John in Kirkby Stephen in a couple of days they looked quite concerned. Based on their hiking experience they didn't think I had left enough walking time to make our rendezvous on time. We pulled out the maps. Clearly they were right. No matter how I looked at it, it was a three day hike to Kirkby Stephen and I only had two before John was scheduled to arrive. Hmm. That was a bit of a dilemma.

There were two factors working in my favour. Osmotherly lies on the eastern side of the Vale of York – the vast area of flat land between the Moors and the Pennines – and a bus to Richmond was due any minute. I made a snap decision, pulled stuff together and scurried out to the bus stop.

I spent the whole trip to Richmond looking out of the window feeling rather pleased that I had miscalculated. The lowland terrain of farm land, small villages and minor roads was nice enough, but it wasn't the kind of terrain I was interested in hiking through, even at the expense of cutting a hole in my Coast-to-Coast journey. I'm not one of those who feels you have to have trodden every inch of a route for the trip to have been worthwhile - or at least, that's how I justify it to myself.

I had heard that Richmond was an attractive town but it exceeded my expectations. To be sure of my timing, I had decided to continue by bus as far as Reeth so I had plenty of time to explore the market square part of the town, with its broad cobbled streets and high Georgian commercial buildings which ring the square and surround the former Trinity Church - now a museum. After a walk around I ended up sitting on my bag in front of the Red Lion, watching the endless parade of cars and people making their way in and out of the square.

The bus to Reeth was small and cramped, but everyone was in good spirits. I got the impression that most of the passengers were returning home after a morning's shopping in the 'big town' and knew each other and the driver well. Nevertheless, they made room for me and my rucksack without complaint and the attractive drive passed quickly. From what I could see through the window, the walk from Richmond to Reeth would have been a pleasant hike along the valley of the River Swale and I was sorry to have missed it. But......well, sometimes you just have to make compromises and this was the price.

Reeth to Keld

Reeth is a 'honeypot' - one of those places which attracts hoards of people because of its location and beauty. Its strategic position at the junction of Arkle Beck and the Swale Valley and close to the edge of the Yorkshire Dales, guarantees plenty of visitors. Surprisingly, it was relatively quiet when I arrived and there were many unfilled parking spaces along the cobbled edges of the village green. To my delight, public toilets lay just across from where the bus had dropped me. I had foolishly quenched my thirst in Richmond and had suffered for it for most of the bus trip.

After replenishing my food supplies at the bakery, I headed west again, up a narrow, stone wall-lined path which climbed steadily up the valley side. It was more of a stream than a path. Water steadily flowed down the middle, washing over the corpses of a number of rabbits in various states of decay. I wondered whether they were casualties of a

Myxomatosis outbreak, or the victims of some teenager with a pellet gun. Either way, I was glad I hadn't thought to refill my water bottle further downstream.

This part of Yorkshire is a pastoral landscape, with dry stone wall enclosed green sheep pastures extending up the valley sides to the edge of the moor. The hills are low and rounded and only the upper parts are clad in heather and bracken. Across the valley, smoke was pouring from large fires where heather was being burned to promote new growth for better grazing for sheep and grouse, but my side of the valley was mercifully free of such dangers.

My route followed an old mine road leading to the remains of the Old Gang Lead Smelting Mill, an impressive collection of chimneys, ruined walls, old buildings and slag heaps. For miles around, the hills have been sculpted, dug, churned and mined so that little of the natural contour of the hills remains. This was mining on a vast industrial scale and must have employed hundreds, if not thousands of people at its peak. In places, the toxins left over from mining and smelting still prevent natural vegetation growth, although in most areas the heather does a reasonably good job of obscuring the scars on the landscape and creates the illusion of 'natural'.

I had started to become conscious of a dull ache in my left heel. I like to blame my relatively new boots, but the reality is, I just hadn't got my body well enough prepared before leaving home. So far I've managed to escape many of the physical problems that affect people my age, and have a tendency to assume I can behave as if I am still in my twenties. Sometimes my body reminds me that I can't.

The steep descent down the side of the Gunnerside Gill valley, over talus and old mining debris, didn't help my ankle at all, especially when I stepped on a loose boulder and gave my Achilles tendon a tweak. I walked the last few miles with a bit of a limp.

The village of Keld is a tiny fragment of its former self. Once housing up to 6000 lead mine workers, there can't be more than a hundred permanent residents now, who are vastly outnumbered by tourists and hikers during the holiday season. Keld lies at the intersection of the Pennine Way and the Coast-to-Coast Walk, so sees more than its fair share of hikers. But a gloomy Thursday in mid-March hardly counts as holiday season in most people's book and the place seemed deserted when I arrived. I was aiming for the Keld Lodge – a former youth hostel, now converted to a hotel and restaurant. I'd enjoyed my stay there while hiking the Pennine Way a couple of years before and had my mind set on a nice pint and a good, hot meal.

As I walked up the little road towards the lodge, I met a lady working in her garden. After the usual pleasantries, she asked me where I was heading, then told me that the lodge was closed. It looked as though I would be rolling out my bivvy once again. With my tendon beginning to throb, I was not looking forward to having to walk too much further to find a suitable spot.

"Are there any B&B's open?" I asked.

She assured me there were not, but.....

"You could try the Butt House. They sometimes take people out of season."

It was only a very short walk to the Butt House - a fine, sturdy looking stone house on the edge of the village. I banged on the door, and after a short while, a rather startled looking guy answered.

"I know it's out of season, but would you have a room for the night?"

Chris checked with his wife and they concluded they could cope with me, muddy boots and all. Sometimes luck just seems to be on one's side. Chris and Jacquie were extraordinarily good hosts, great company and superb cooks. And they had beer!

Kirkby Stephen

The next day was cool and damp - perfect temperature for the walk along the narrow road which parallels the Swale valley. After crossing a narrow stone bridge, my path gradually climbed out of the valley, following the eastern edge of the Whitsundale Beck to the farm at Ravenseat then up the Ney Gill valley on to Birkdale Common. After leaving the farm, the wind had picked up considerably. By the time I made it to the tin sheet covered safety hut at the end of the valley, making progress had become quite difficult. It was a great relief to be able to sit out of the wind for a while. If conditions had been really poor, that hut could easily be a life saver.

I was far from in trouble though, so after some water and a snack, I closed the door behind me and set off up the hill towards the Nine Standards Rigg. My limp was becoming a bit more pronounced but with no-one to complain to, I stumped along across the soggy moors towards the summit. Nine Standards Rigg was the highest point on the hike so far. At 662 metres (2171 feet) above sea level, it isn't particularly high, but with strong winds, low cloud and a grey day, it felt remote and wild, although the numerous boot prints in the soft muddy peat at the summit showed that it was a popular destination. As I headed across the boggy plain between the trig point and the cairns after which the Nine Standards is named, two middle-aged hikers appeared out of the mist. Under such circumstances, it's common for people to share a quick word about the weather or the hiking conditions but I received nothing more than a cursory, and decidedly dismissive grunt of acknowledgement before they disappeared behind me.

The Nine Standards were well worth the struggle. Nine beautifully constructed dry-stone cairns are arranged in a line along the broad ridge. They are all slightly different shapes: conical, stepped, simple pillars and are surprisingly eerie, looming out of the mist.

I saw no more people until I was almost at Kirkby Stephen. The track up from the village was well worn, but there was no-one on it today. About half-way down, I stopped at a small wooden bridge which had been constructed to cross a particularly boggy piece of ground. As I was clambering across it, I slipped, my pack unbalanced me and I ended up teetering on the rail, not sure whether I would fall face first into the pool below, or regain my footing. It was like something out of the final scene of the original '*The Italian Job*'. Fortunately I prevailed, but in stretching to counter balance I had tweaked my achilles again. By the time I got to the hostel in Kirkby Stephen, I was hobbling.

It was a good job that John's train wasn't due to arrive until the next afternoon. It gave me almost a full day to relax and heal. Little did I know how long that healing process would actually take. I was having a hard time just making my way up and down the stairs in the hostel. My left foot felt as though it was locked at 90 degrees to my leg. Every little movement hurt. It was increasingly sore to the touch.

The Kirkby Stephen railway station lies a couple of miles to the south of the town. I left my gear at the hostel and giving myself plenty of time for a leisurely walk, ambled - or more accurately, hobbled - down the path which parallels the busy road. The station was deserted and lovely. It had been restored in 2005 by the Settle and Carlisle Railway Trust and despite the passage of ten years, the paint was still gleaming and the whole place was spotless. Unfortunately, they'd forgotten to turn on the heat in the waiting room and it got a bit chilly as I sat on a cold bench until the train arrived. John's train finally rolled in on the far platform. I didn't see him until he was already half way across the elegant cast iron footbridge.

It's an odd thing, but when you haven't seen someone for a couple of years, there is always that very slight, nagging anxiety that you might not recognize them or they would be somehow different to the way they are in your memory. But of course I recognized him. He was the guy in hiking gear, carrying a rucksack and the only person to get off the train. He was just the same as ever. We went straight to the pub in Nateby.

Hiking with John

During the night, the temperature dropped and it started to snow. A fine skim of the sloppy, wet stuff was on the ground as we left Kirkby Stephen. The air was clear and cool and my rucksack was feeling lighter than usual. We had decided that camping would be out on this leg of the trip, so with the approval of Denise at the hostel, I had cached some of my gear, reducing weight and bulk considerably.

We left Kirkby Stephen along a minor road but soon turned off for an indistinct path across the snow covered fields. As always, John tromped along, never bothered by the steepness of the climb or the slippery footing, while I explored the lower reaches of my lungs and struggled to stay vertical. My ankle was decidedly sore for the first couple of miles, but gradually the pain drifted out of my consciousness as the wind picked up and the snow became a little deeper. In many ways it was a magnificent day. Patches of blue sky would suddenly appear between the dark grey clouds, then just as soon vanish as another snow squall hit. At times, we had wonderful views through clear air across to the Lake District; at others we could barely see fifty yards ahead or keep our footing as the wind tried to tear us from the hillside. Fortunately, those squalls were rare and for most of the time we were able to plod ever westward heading in to the prevailing wind, for our evening destination at Shap.

We hadn't really made any plans for lunch but after twelve miles of fairly tough going, both of us were ready to sit down somewhere warm with something to eat. The pub at Orton seemed the obvious choice. Depressingly, it was closed, although the tea room attached to the Kennedy's Chocolate Shop was open. Dripping pools of water from our sodden boots, we lingered over mugs of coffee and cake. It wasn't perfect, but far, far better than nothing.

The last half-a-dozen miles to Shap were a bit of a slog - at least for me - with the weather alternating between clear and cold and windy and snowy. John's aged hiking boots were beginning to fail him. The material at the heel was worn through, leaving a sharp edge which had cut a nasty hole in his heel. We attempted a patch it with some moleskin, but it didn't really help and John soldiered along without any complaint or external signs of pain. Damn! How could I continue to whine when he showed no signs of distress from a much more obvious injury?

As daylight began to fade, we crossed the bridge over the M6 and headed into the village, joining the main road almost opposite the King's Arms Hotel. There was no question in my mind about what would happen next. I had little interest in going any further. If they had a room, beer and some food that would do for me. John had other plans though. While I went inside and ordered two pints, he went on a scouting expedition around the village to see what other options there might be as the hotel bar was sterile and uninteresting, the food looked ordinary and the prices I was quoted for a room were unappealing. I drank my first pint while I tapped into the hotel's WiFi and sent a quick email home. Then I drank the pint I had bought for John.

I was just thinking about ordering a third when John returned with a strange story of finding a B&B run by an elderly, bearded lady, heating herself by a single bar electric fire. I pictured a musty, damp, worker's cottage, smelling profoundly of old lady and wet dog, with two tiny beds crammed into the long-ago-left-home son's former bedroom. Not that I cared much by this point - lead on John.

The reality was very different. We entered a vast, 17th century house, with carved, wood-panelled hall walls, stained glass, flag-stone floors and elegant furnishings. We were shown to a delightful, warm bedroom with a beautifully appointed bathroom with masses of hot water and clean, fluffy towels. Our 'elderly lady' wasn't particularly old and certainly didn't have a beard. She apologized for not being able to cook us an evening meal because she had to go out to a parish council meeting. No - not the picture I had conjured at all!

After a relaxing night, breakfast was equally magnificent. Our host brought out an enormous plate of toast, bacon, eggs, home-made Cumberland sausages, fried tomatoes, mushrooms etc. etc. - far more than we could possibly eat, all washed down with plenty of coffee and juice.

Kidsty Pike to Grasmere

About three miles west of Shap we left the rounded hills behind and entered the craggy, precipitous world of the Lake District. We had passed Shap Abbey, crossed a sturdy stone bridge over Swindale Beck and were soon walking along the lake shore path on the north side of Hawkeswater Reservoir. The views along the lake are truly lovely, but the way the surrounding hills slope straight into the water jangles the mind. There is no harmony between the water and the land. There are no natural shores; it just looks wrong. I later learned that originally there had been two smaller lakes, but the dam had raised the water levels by 95 feet, joining them together into a single, four mile long reservoir supplying water for Manchester. The raised water levels flooded the villages of Mardale Green and Measand and filled up the valley. Not surprisingly, locals were not generally in favour of the project, but in 1929, common folk had little say in the matter.

There was plenty of snow on the surrounding hills as we made our way along the lake shore path. Whenever blue sky was visible, the water was a startlingly blue, but it quickly turned to grey whenever the cloud cover was complete. Across the tops of the surrounding hills, snow squalls whipped the surface snow into spindrift.

Down at lake level, we were sheltered from the wind. We passed the fresh corpse of a deer, lying right in the middle of the path in the snow. A few yards later on, we came across a second deer, swimming just off shore in the lake.

From near the southern end of Haweswater, our route climbed abruptly on to Kidsty Howes, Kidsty Pike, then on along the ridge to Patterdale. We had noticed the spin-drift blowing across the mountain tops, but I don't think either of us was quite prepared for the brutal conditions we encountered. The first problem was that the deep snow had completely buried any signs of a path. John had been navigating with the maps in his guide book, while I had been double-checking from time to time with the GPS and maps on my phone. Without a clear path to guide us, we used them to keep on track as we climbed steadily from the lake.

At times the snow was almost waist deep; we were in constant danger of twisting an ankle on the rugged ground beneath the snow. Luckily, I was wearing gaiters, so my feet stayed relatively dry but John's rain pants didn't cover his boots and the snow kept packing in between his feet and the boots. His feet were soaked and cold within minutes.

While trudging up the steep slope to Kidsty Howes was difficult enough, it did nothing to prepare us for the grind up Kidsy Pike. By now, the wind had really started to howl, picking up clouds of icy spin drift and hurling them in our faces. If it had been difficult to keep our footing before, now we were frequently brought to a complete stand-still by the wind blasting down the slope, which threatened to blow us right off the mountain. The climb had made me sweat heavily. My inner clothes were soaking and rapidly becoming chilled. My legs were shaky from the effort, my ankle hurt, my breath was gone.

There were times during that climb when part of me wanted to either just give up and sink down into a nice warm nest in the snow, or beat a retreat down to the relatively safety of the lake shore. I don't know whether John was feeling much better - he had certainly resorted to putting on his gloves and extra jacket before we reached the summit, but his feet must have felt like blocks of ice. We slowly inched our way forward.

When I had flown out of Canada, we had been experiencing normal weather for February; very cold, with still, clear days and even colder nights. Generally it would only snow when the temperature rose above -10c, which it rarely did. I had been spending plenty of hours outside in these conditions and was well used to bitter cold, but without the wind, it seemed balmy compared to the weather on Kidsy Pike.

Eventually we made the summit but there was no time for celebration or rejoicing. I'd had enough of being blown around and chilled. I suggested that instead of following the ridge, we bailed out straight down the Hayeswater Gill valley then follow the road to Patterdale. The Youth Hostel was at the outskirts of the village. It was warm, they had beer, the White Lion just down the road served a decent meal. All was good again.

After a mild night most of the snow was gone from the lower slopes. This day promised to be a relatively easy one; just an amble up Grisedale up to Grisedale Tarn, then a quick drop down the other side to Grasmere. That suited me just fine. I was looking forward to a short, easy day to give my throbbing ankle a bit of a rest.

The walk up Grisedale was an easy stroll along a farm road which hugged the side of the valley, before climbing steeply up to Ruthwaite Lodge - a former mining hut where we rested for a few moments. Perching my camera on my hiking pole, I took a picture of the two of us sitting on the bench outside. John looks relaxed and fresh as he studies the guide book. I look exhausted!

Ruthwaite Lodge lay just below the snow line, although on this day, the presence of snow made little difference, as long as we watched for hidden crevices between the rocks. For once, the wind wasn't howling and we made good progress past the tarn, over the pass and down into the next valley. Despite the Lake District's reputation as being over crowded, we had seen few people and those we did see looked as though they knew their business and were properly dressed for the conditions. At least, that was the case until we got to Grasmere.

Grasmere is a small, busy village, just up the road from Ambleside. Even this early in the season, it was crawling with people who seemed to be wandering around with no real purpose, other than to gaze in the few shop windows and perhaps buy an ice cream to eat on a bench in the central green - as long as they could find one that wasn't already occupied. As we walked, John quoted me a fact he'd picked up from somewhere, which suggested that most visitors to the Lake District never stray more than 400 yards from their vehicle. Certainly, at this time of year there were many people in the villages and only a handful in the hills. After a brief stop in a distinctly unsatisfying hotel bar, John and I joined the wanderers to find something to eat. We had time to kill before the youth hostel opened for the day.

Ouch!

Our passage across the Lake District was becoming a bit routine. Each day we would start off from a valley, follow a stream valley until the stream petered out at a high pass, cross the pass (usually in the wind and snow) then drop down into the next main valley for the night. This day would be no exception. The kindly lad manning the office at the Grasmere youth hostel phoned ahead to book our stay at the Borrowdale Youth Hostel in Rosthwaite. As long as we were able to get our bodies there, we had a guaranteed place to rest our heads.

Over night, almost all the snow had disappeared from the lower slopes and apart from a few patches in the hollows, it was almost gone from the hilltops too. The path up the Far Easedale Gill valley was well defined and pleasant, with berry-laden Holly trees and moss covered stone walls along the creek. The bracken and heather clad hillsides were dotted with small, scruffy, hardy-looking Herdwick sheep which were either so used to hikers or so self-possessed that they hardly bothered to lift their heads as we passed.

The long haul up to Greenup Edge was tiring but without the tearing winds or blowing snow we had experienced on other passes, it seemed benign and pleasant. It was still cool and damp though, so managing body temperature was my greatest difficulty. It didn't seem to affect John much – I think he just opened the vents on his hiking trousers to shed a little heat - but during the steep climbs I would have to shed outer clothing to prevent myself from sweating too much or over-heating.

Then, as soon as the climbing was over, I would have to layer up again, to stop myself from getting chilled. It's a good job John is a patient chap. He had already had to adjust his natural pace to accommodate my limping gait. Now he had to wait while I fussed with clothing or stopped to take pictures as well. Complaints? Not once!

I don't want this to sound like one long whining session, but my achilles tendon was really starting to be a bit of a nuisance. Perhaps if I had given it a chance to rest once it had started to hurt, it would have been fine. But I didn't. By now I had walked about 80 miles of fairly rough country on it, and it was letting me know. To make matters worse, by favouring my left leg I was starting to feel a sympathetic twinge in my right hip.

We crested Greenup Edge and started the descent towards Rosthwaite, past the rocky outcrops of Lining Crag and Eagle Crag. All things considered, I was doing rather well until I started down a particularly rocky section around Eagle Crag. I stepped off a flat wet rock and misjudged the distance to the next one, ending up with just the very tip of my boot on the rock and my heel in a hollow with my full weight on it. I'm embarrassed to admit that I screamed out like a little girl as a searing pain shot up my leg and I collapsed in a heap on the rocks. For one horrible second, I thought I'd snapped my achilles tendon - I'd already had that experience with the other leg, a few years earlier - so I quickly checked to see if I could move my foot. Instead of hanging there like a dead fish as it would if the tendon had completely separated, it would still move. I hadn't snapped it, but I think I must have torn it a bit. It took a while before I felt ready to continue, and when I did I was rather more careful for the rest of the descent.

The long haul down to the valley bottom wasn't much fun, but at least John didn't have to help me off the mountain. After a while, the pain became mere background noise and I was able to hobble along without looking or feeling too crippled. We made straight for the Langthwaite Country Inn in Stonethwaite which was open, welcoming and had a big fire going in the fireplace.

I'm having trouble remembering the sequence of events now - perhaps they were cloudy in my mind at the time - but somehow we ended up in the bar at the back of the Scafell Hotel in Rosthwaite, where we met two very pleasant hikers we had encountered on the hills shortly after I had my fall. They were easy company and the drinks started to flow well as we swapped tall tales of the hills. It was probably a good thing that they had a firm dinner date with their spouses, so we were only mildly plastered when we arrived at the Borrowdale Youth Hostel.

The hostel was crowded. A number of school parties were using it as a base for explorations in the surrounding area. I found the kid's excitement and enthusiasm infectious and for once, didn't long for a quiet spot free from chatter and clamour. Only one other person was sharing our room so we were insulated from their noise and activity once it was time for bed. I did feel for him though; I am a bit of a snorer, especially after a few drinks. I hope he was a deep sleeper.

Seatoller, Black Sail and Ennerdale

It's a long slog up the steep road from Seatoller to the Honister Pass Slate Mine and John left me in the metaphorical dust. One of the good things about hiking with a friend is that there is no need to be in constant conversation or to walk at the same pace. If one person goes on ahead, it doesn't mean they're in a snit. John was full of beans and was enjoying stretching out; I was walking through molasses and breathing hard.

From the top of the pass, our route followed an old mine track above Honister Crag before turning south towards Grey Knotts and the descent into Ennerdale. Looking back, we could see the old mine workings carved in to the side of the valley and the piles of waste material spreading down the hillside beneath the mine shaft entrances. These hills must be riddled with holes.

Little snow remained on the hilltops, but the cloud base was brushing the highest peaks and the wind was constant and strong. I set my camera to record some video; John has a bandanna across his face and the top of his hood is flapping wildly. Our voices are completely drowned out by the roar of the wind. The wind rushing up the end of the valley was particularly strong. We had to descend between bursts which threatened to blow us off our feet or back up the slope.

Further down the valley, the wind calmed enough to make walking feel more normal. I think both of us were holding on to the fantasy that the Black Sail Hut Youth Hostel would be open, that we would be welcomed inside and provided with a nice cup of sugary hot tea. But it was not to be. The hut was deserted and locked. Black Sail is a former shepherd's bothy and one of Britain's most remote youth hostels. It lies amid majestic scenery and has a history of providing accommodation for some of Britain's most famous climbers. But not for us. After a brief break, we headed on down the path.

The next few miles were along a road through Ennerdale Forest – a substantial plantation which occupies the lower slopes of both sides of the valley. It was uninspiring walking, but glimpses of the high crags on either side, and John's running commentary of which famous climbers had climbed what and when made it more interesting. Eventually we arrived at Gillerthwaite where yet another youth hostel failed to welcome us with open arms and a fresh pot of tea. We resigned ourselves to a quick snack in their front yard before heading along the path on the south side of Ennerdale Water.

Ennerdale Water is only about 2 miles long but it is stunningly beautiful. We weren't seeing it under the best conditions; the weather was raw and damp with a strong wind whipping the surface of the lake into white-caps, but nothing could detract from it's majesty. The path clings to the southern shore through old forest, sloping pasture and across the heights at Angler's Crag. It's a lovely walk along a lovely lake shore – a fitting end to our passage through the Lake District.

As usual, our first destination in Ennerdale Bridge was the pub. It didn't take long to establish that there was no room at the Fox and Hounds as they were in the middle of renovations, and I was a bit wary of the Shepherds Arms Hotel as I had read their rates on-line and they seemed a bit pricey. John still had energy to burn, so while I nursed a pint and read a motorcycle magazine at the Fox, he wandered off around the village looking for alternative accommodation.

It was a three pint wander. He returned with stories of closed B&B's, of places under construction, of semi-hostile owners and disappointment. Not wanting to walk further, we asked the bar lady whether she could think of anything.

"Have you tried the Shepherds? They should have a room or two free".

I explained that they seemed a bit expensive, but was quickly assured that I must have been looking at the high season rates and that out-of-season rates were much more reasonable. We tried the Shepherds. The rates were fine. It was pleasant, warm, comfortable and served beer and food – excellent!

On to St. Bees

Having left the Lake District behind, it felt as though the hike was really over with nothing left to do but walk the few miles to St. Bees and catch the train back to John's home near Halifax. I had an appointment in Cowling to pick up a rental motorbike the next day, so I was quite eager to get this last day over and done. I have no doubt we missed some interesting hill walking but we chose to stick to the road to Cleator Moor then follow an almost straight line to St. Bees, missing out the cliff walk around St. Bees Head.

I really don't like having to meet schedules, but it's an occupational hazard if you have a limited time to do all the things you want to do and a plane to catch at the end of it. During the next week I had promised myself some motorcycle riding in the Pennines and Wales, a quick visit with my brother and family in Birmingham, and my customary visit to see old friends in Norfolk.

Walking down the A5086 between Cleator Moor and Cleator left me in little doubt that we had forsaken the world of honey-pots and were back into the grimy world of industrial Britain. This used to be iron mining country; it shows in the bleak terraced houses and the general air of despondency. The grey drizzly weather may not of been helping, but I have the feeling it would look much the same in bright sunshine. Although the Sellafield nuclear complex has now taken up some of the slack, the decline of mining and its associated industries has left a high rate of unemployment.

We walked on, passing a sign indicating two and a half miles to St. Bees. As we headed west on the road out of Bigrigg - sounding more like something out of an American road movie than a village name - we encountered a lady walking her German Shepherd dog. The dog couldn't wait to get at us, straining vigorously on it's leash. Dogs aren't good liars. We could tell from its body language that it really just wanted a cuddle, not a chunk of flesh. While we took turns to pet the dog, we chatted about German Shepherds (I was missing mine) and how so many people shy away from them, when really, they are wonderful and reliable friends.

As we entered the village of St. Bees, two heavily laden hikers were heading up the hill towards us, just starting their eastward trek along the Coast to Coast Walk. They had all manner of stuff hanging from their packs; water bottles, camp stoves, formal tea services (yes, I'm kidding!). I could see from the look on John's face that he was thinking the same as me; how long would it be before they realised they were carrying far too much and started to litter the trail with abandoned equipment.

The way I was hobbling, I was glad to be done. John was all set to explore the village but I suggested we head straight for the railway station instead. I was looking forward to a relaxing evening back at John's house and picking up the motorcycle in the morning for the next stage of my adventure.

2nd Bivvy, Fylingdale Moor

Actually, I'm English

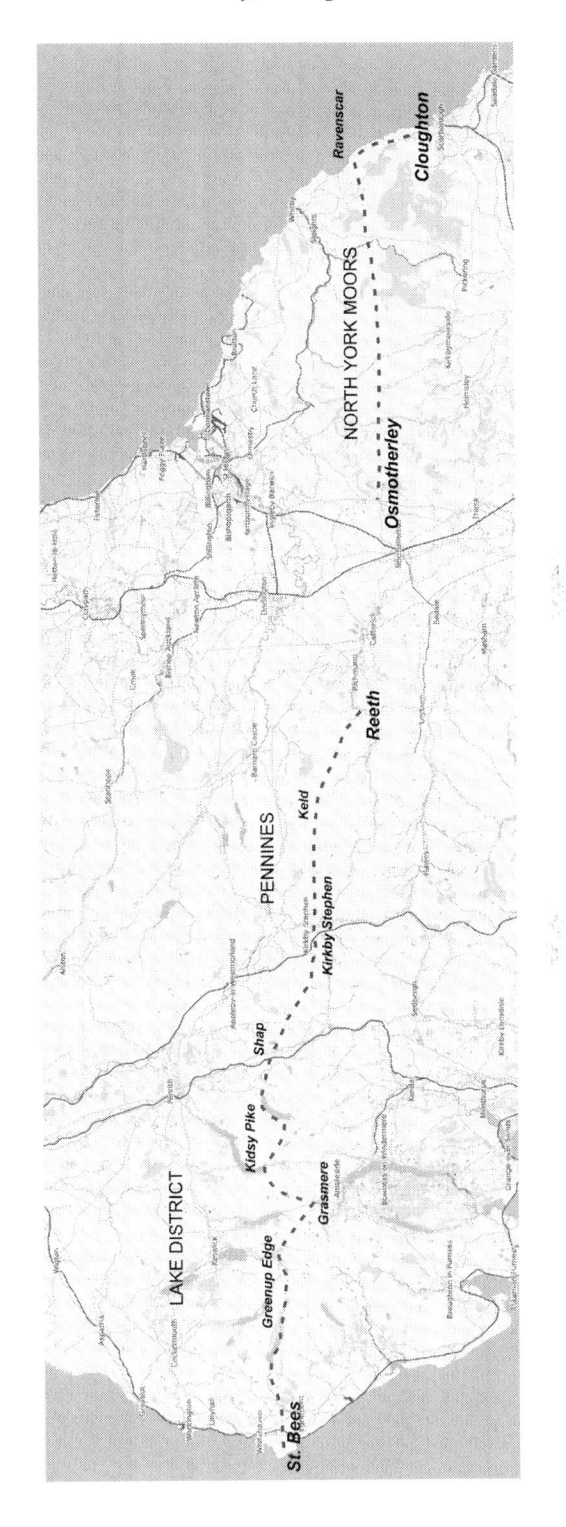

Nick Adams

Path of Dead Rabbits

Lead mining country between Reeth and Keld

Actually, I'm English

A brief rest on the way to Nine Standards

Dead deer on the path - Hawkeswater

PART 6

BACK ON THE BIKE
ANOTHER ROYAL ENFIELD

D&C

Once again I had opted to rent a Royal Enfield. The many rental places I found on the internet offered the usual crop of BMWs, Triumphs and Hondas, but none of them appealed to me: too modern, too sophisticated, no charisma. I wasn't interested in speed or digital displays. I needed the steady, plodding charm of an old fashioned slogger – one that was just modern enough that it wouldn't break down in the rain or drip oil.

After a good deal of intenet digging, I found D&C Classic Motor Cycles in Cowling, Yorkshire who were prepared to rent me a suitable bike. Cowling is only 20 miles north of John's house near Halifax and since he was happy to run me up there at the conclusion of our hike, it seemed a perfect fit.

Ironically, I had passed D&C's place in 2012 while I was walking the Pennine Way. I remember seeing the Royal Enfield sign above their workshop door and must have filed it away in some dark recess of my mind for future use, so when it was time for John and I to head to Cowling, I knew exactly where to go.

From the outside, D&C is not the most prepossessing place of business. Their workshop is part of an old mill complex of dark stone and corrugated metal doors. At first I couldn't find an entrance or raise any one from within, but after a few minutes, a voice from inside directed me to a door around the back and I was ushered upstairs to Dave's somewhat chaotic office. I must admit that for a few moments I wondered what I had got myself in to, but it didn't take long to realise that despite appearances, Dave had everything sorted out, the bike was ready and I just needed to sign a few papers that were somewhere on his crowded desk. While Dave photocopied my driver's licence and completed a few other administrative tasks, I scratched his dog Scamp's ears and hoped that the bike was in better condition than some of the off-road clothing hanging from the pegs behind me.

On the road again

I shouldn't have worried. The riding gear was loan stuff from off-road tours that Dave leads through the Yorkshire countryside. The Royal Enfield he led me to was spotless, almost new, and not only equipped with a set of leather panniers, but a top box almost big enough to hide in. After a quick tour of the bike, he gave me an enormous chain and padlock, wished me well and left me alone to get packed, dressed and ready for the road.

After my experiences with the weather last time, I had brought rather more cold weather gear with me. It wasn't motorcycle clothing, since, as before, it had to be light enough do double duty for hiking, but it was warm and waterproof. At least, I thought it was.

I had barely been on the road for ten minutes when it started to rain. I mean really rain. My plan was to head north up to Kirkby Stephen to retrieve the camping gear I had left at the youth hostel, before heading across to the Lake District to ride through that lovely landscape. By the time I reached Earby I could feel a trickle of water on my thighs. By Hellifield my knees were wet and cold. By Settle, my so-called waterproof rain pants had let so much water through that I was soaked from the waist down. My gore-tex rain jacket was doing a sterling job of keeping my top half dry, and I had had the good sense to wear my hiking gaiters, so the road splash was unable to trickle down to my boots and chill my feet, but my rain pants were a disaster - they had to go.

I found a parking space across from the Old Naked Man Café and walked stiff-legged to the Cave and Crag outdoors shop next door. I left a puddle on the floor as I explained my predicament to the shop keeper and asked her advise about something genuinely waterproof. She managed to talk me out of buying the cheapest pull-ons, steering me instead to some higher quality rain pants with full length zippers. I am in her debt! They have lived up to every bit of her sales talk, exceeded my expectations and have been worth every penny.

Taking advantage of her changing room, I removed my sodden

trousers, pulled on some thermal underwear, a fresh pair of trousers and my new, crisp rain pants. I was ready for the road again.

The road from Settle, through Horton-in-Ribblesdale and up the Widdale valley to Hawes must be a delightful ride in good weather. It was a pleasant enough ride in the pouring rain, with the hills shrouded in cloud, the water streaming off the hills and the puddles accumulating on the road. I was enjoying myself. The bike was chugging along nicely, feeling predictable and secure, despite the wet roads and potentially slippery conditions. Now that my legs were dry, my thoughts turned to my hands which were wet and cold. This was a great source of disappointment. Before leaving Canada, I had agonized over which gloves to bring and had spent many fruitless hours searching for something that would be suitable for hiking yet robust and waterproof enough for use while riding. I finally settled on a pair of snow-boarding mittens, with an insulated fleece inner glove and a waterproof outer. They lied. They were not waterproof. They leaked like a sieve!

By the time I got to Hawes the rain was still hammering down and I was more than ready for a break. The Old Board Inn offered sandwiches, beer and a hot fire in the hearth to warm my gloves and my shivering body. I had hardly stripped off my gear and ordered a pint before I was joined in the bar by two travellers who, if anything, looked as though they needed the fireplace more than I did. I think they were Japanese, but since they had about as much English as I had Japanese (which was nil) our communication was limited to smiles and nods. How they managed to order something to eat is still a puzzle too me, but they stayed close to the fire as if they'd just come in from the Arctic.

Eventually it was time for me to get back on the road. It was still raining, my gloves were still sodden - although for a few minutes at least, they had a comforting wet warmth - but I was happy to be rolling again. It's a curious thing, but I really quite enjoy riding in the rain and I don't mind being a bit damp and even a bit chilly, as long as there is the possibility of a warm bed and dry clothes somewhere in my future.

The first few miles were along the main road west towards Sedbergh, before I turned north on the B road to Kirkby Stephen. This was moorland country. The road is lined with dry stone walls and hugs the valley of the River Eden which tumbles down towards the town. Looking at the map now, I see that the upper edge of the fells are lined with crags, but I saw nothing of Wild Boar Fell or Hangingstone Scar; they were hidden in the mist.

Despite the rain, I stopped to take a couple of pictures at Pendragon Castle – a picturesque 12th century ruin – before heading north again through Nateby, where John and I had shared a pint, then on into Kirkby

Stephen. It was raining so hard that I kept my helmet on when I banged on the hostel door, so I suppose I shouldn't have been too surprised by Denise's somewhat guarded reaction. Fortunately she quickly recognised me and invited me in for a chance to dry off and warm up, but I explained that since I was wet already, I'd rather just keep going while I had daylight in my favour. I gathered my camping gear from where she had stored it, thanked her once again, and headed back to the bike. Whether it made any sense or not, I thought if I continued to head west, I would outrun this rain.

Fat chance! By the time I reached the M6 at Tebay, the rain was undiminished. I joined the traffic heading south, riding along in the slow lane, getting drenched in the road spray of every vehicle that passed. I stuck to a steady 60mph. Inevitably, I was about the slowest thing moving. Somehow I managed to completely miss the intersection to Kendal and was at the Killington Lake Services before I realised I had gone too far. Oh well, I needed fuel and something to eat anyway.

When I came back out, it was still pouring. I splashed the water off the seat with my wet glove, turned the key, hit the starter button...........and nothing happened. Ignition on - check, side stand up – check. I hit the starter button again - nothing. I worked around the bike checking everything I could think of, giving all the wires a wiggle, before going back inside to buy a can of WD40 to douse the electrics. I doused the electrics, gave it a few more seconds then.....nothing. In desperation, I tried a bump start, but my damaged achilles tendon didn't appreciate it much and I couldn't get any momentum. The rain continued to batter my helmet as I sat wondering what to do next.

Then lightning struck. Not literal lightning - just the kind that goes off in your head when you realise that you have been really, really stupid. I turned the key, pulled in the clutch and hit the starter button. The Enfield whirred into life and settled into a nice steady idle while I felt like a complete idiot. I clicked the gear lever until the little green 'neutral' light showed and gently let out the clutch. The bike continued to run. I turned it off, turned it back on, hit the starter and it started, instantly...........duh! I had forgotten that most modern motorcycles won't start if they are in gear unless the clutch is pulled in. It's a safety thing to stop you jerking off down the road uncontrollably.

I was heading in the general direction of Grizebeck, a small village on the south-western edge of the Lake District. Before flying to the UK I had posted a query to the 'RealClassic' forum. I had been having trouble deciding how to dovetail my hiking with motorcycle riding and was looking for advise. Quite a few people responded, including Simon, who wrote "If you're up this way......." no doubt never thinking for one second that I'd actually turn up. I arrived to find him not at home and the pub opposite closed and under construction. I backtracked a few miles to a pub in Spark Bridge. It had been a long, cold day.

Lake District Redux

By morning the weather had changed. The sky was clear and while the roads were still damp from yesterday's rain, they were no longer awash, so I retraced my steps to Grizebeck where, this time, Simon was home. Within a very short time I realised that we shared a lot in common. Our conversation soon ranged far beyond our mutual interest in motorbikes and I would have been happy to chat for longer, but he had work on his house to get on with and I had a date with some northern roads.

When travelling alone my moods can fluctuate wildly. I usually spend more time surfing the wave than below it, but just once in a while the wave will catch me unawares and I will start to gasp for air. Today was one of those days. For no good reason I was in the doldrums. The weather was fine, the roads were relatively uncluttered, I was happy with the bike and the scenery was incomparable. The problem was with me, and there wasn't too much I could do about that.

I had intended to head towards Eskdale then take the Hardnott and Wrynose Passes towards Windermere and Ambleside. But for some inexplicable reason, I found myself rolling along the A 593 towards Coniston instead. I'd been looking forward to Hardnott Pass. Back in 1983, Chris and I had ridden up it during a month long motorcycle tour of England on a Honda 250. More accurately, I rode up it! There were a few places where the pass was so steep that the poor little bike simply couldn't carry the two of us and all our gear. Chris had to walk. When I describe it like this, it doesn't sound very chivalrous.

I'm still not sure why I turned towards Coniston. I don't even think it was a map reading error. It just happened. One minute I was heading for Eskdale, the next I was on the A593. Almost before I knew it, I was passing through Ambleside heading north towards Rydal and Thirlmere. On foot, the Lake District had seemed huge; on the bike, I was through it and heading east on the Penrith Road before I had much of a chance to blink. Why I didn't spend a day or two exploring the Lake District's wonderful secondary roads, I have no idea. I think something in me must just have shut down for a while. It still baffles me.

I have another theory about why I abandoned the Lake District so soon - three actually - none of which make much sense. I had never spent much time in the Lake District when I lived in the UK, so it didn't feel like part of the 'home' I had been exploring on my various trips. Having spent the past week or more hiking through it in some admittedly difficult circumstances and weather, no matter how nice the scenery and how pleasant the riding, it just wasn't as engaging. And lastly - and this is probably closest to the truth - I was starting to feel the time before my return flight ebbing away. I still had many places to go and people to visit, and only a few days within which to do it.

One of those things was to have lunch in the Tan Hill pub. If you've already laboured through the Pennine Way chapter above, you'll remember that I stopped there briefly during my walk. It's the highest pub in Britain and has become something of a Mecca for motorcyclists. It's not that it's difficult to get to or that the roads demand a high level of rider skill. It's only a few miles off the main road from Brough, but it's high and the network of single track moorland roads which serve it make it feel a bit wild.

Once I turned south at Brough, the road climbed steadily upwards, leaving hedgerows, farms and forest behind as it emerged on to the high moor. Crossing a wet cattle grid while riding one handed and recording video with the other isn't recommended, but I wanted to capture a bit of footage to inflict on friends and family back home. The rear wheel skipped on the wet metal and I was tempted to grab for the bars with my loose hand, but as there were no other vehicles around, I carried on filming.

There were three other motorbikes in the parking area in front of the pub: a Yamaha Tenere and two Honda Africa Twins. Great bikes! These are 'adventure' style bikes with plenty of suspension travel, crash bars and skid plates - bikes on which one could circumnavigate the globe. The riders were deep in conversation, so I ordered a pint and some curry and settled in to a window seat to check my email and communicate with home.

In Canada, the arrival of someone on a heavily laden Royal Enfield would have immediately sparked 'where are you from - where are you heading' curiosity and conversation, but here, I was just another grey hair on an old fashioned bike. I didn't mind. The beer and curry were good.

You might think that motorcycles and pubs are an odd mix. Pubs sell alcoholic beverages while motorcycling demands a high degree of coordination, balance and skill – things that are easily impaired by booze. Yet, as far as I can tell from my many hours spent reading and chatting on British motorcycle internet forums, making a pub a ride destination is completely ordinary. It's true that pubs also sell food and soft drinks but as far as I have been able to observe, a lunch time pint or two is not considered odd or dangerous. A cynic might say it's because the beer is weak and watery – but that's an opinion best not voiced out loud.

From Tan Hill I headed south-east across the moor to Reeth, where I stopped for old time's sake to visit the municipal toilet, then down the east side of the Pennines to Masham. I was rather hoping that the whole town would have the smell of beer mash oozing from the Black Sheep and Theakstons breweries, but if it did, I couldn't detect it. I'm also disappointed to relate that the town's name has nothing to do with beer making. Wikipedia tells me that it's name is Anglo-Saxon, derived from "Mæssa's Ham", the homestead belonging to Mæssa. Boring!

I still had no plans for the day. I was just enjoying riding but as I rode along the long, rather empty stretch west of Pateley Bridge I noticed that the shadows were lengthening. It was time to make some sort of decision about where I was heading. The Youth Hostels at Kettlewell and Malham were possibilities, but either would involved some back-tracking and I had no idea whether they would be open. In the end, I settled for Gargrave.

I have come to realise that I am a creature of habit. There may have been other places to stay, but if there were, I ignored them and headed straight for the Mason's Arms - the pub I'd visited a few years before and described dismissively a couple of chapters ago. In the intervening time, the pub had changed hands and been through some renovations. While the bar décor was still the same, the whole place no longer exuded an air of desperation. The barman / owner told me that a room for the night would be 50 pounds, I could pay in the morning, and if I rode my bike around the back there was secure parking and he'd meet me with the room key. The room was fine - even quite nice.

After a quick shower and change of clothes, I headed back into the village centre to look for something to eat. The bar served food, but I wasn't in the mood for that kind of fare. Instead, almost as if I was following a script, I ambled in to the same Co-op I'd visited before, bought the same pre-packaged sausage rolls, this time with industrial Samosas in a supporting role, and some bottled cider. As before, I sat on the bench outside, traffic watching in the fading light, before heading back to my room to finish off the cider and as many Samosas as I could stomach. I had decided to drop in on my brother and his wife in Birmingham in the morning. That would mean riding through urban traffic for most of the day. I would need all the sleep I could get.

An Urban Day

There was a good frost on the Royal Enfield's seat when I got up. After packing, I walked around trying to find someone to pay, but the doors to the pub were locked and there were no signs of life, so I left the 50 pounds on the bedside table, hoping the cleaning staff were honest, and left.

It was a chilly ride at first, but after Colne I was well into the morning traffic and didn't have time to think about the cold. I think I passed through Burnley, Blackburn and Bolton. Looking at the maze of roads on the map now, I'm not really sure. I passed endless rows of houses, with the tiny walled gardens jammed right up against the street. The few bits of open country were barely noticeable between the long, busy stretches of housing and commercial development, and even where there was open country there were hardly two fields in a row before some sort of house or village. The whole country seemed filled up.

Riding in this kind of urban environment requires a special kind of concentration. Every other vehicle is a potential hazard. There is no room for day-dreaming or taking others actions and reactions for granted. Every fibre of your being has to be alert and vigilant. In Canada, I'm spoiled. The roads I ride are generally traffic free - indeed most of the time there are no other vehicles in sight.

By the time I had navigated through the heart of Manchester and was heading down the A34 towards Stoke-on-Trent, I was perversely starting to enjoy myself. Congleton, Stoke-on-Trent and Stafford blended into each other. I briefly lost the A34 at a roundabout south of Stafford but somehow regained it again above Cannock.

Now, it's a funny thing; although I spent almost all my teenage years in the West Midlands, I had never seen Cannock Chase before. As I rode along, I could see the higher land of forest, farm and heath stretching away to the east. It was attractive enough, but as the closest 'wild' land to Birmingham and Wolverhampton, I shuddered to think how busy the forest trails and paths must be during the weekend.

I barely had enough time to catch a decent breath near Cannock before diving into the chaos of the Birmingham conurbation. I suppose places like Bloxwich, Walsall and West Bromwich have individual identities if you live there, but to me, they were one seamless smear of red brick houses, factories and Asdas.

Navigating through the Birmingham Bull-Ring to Moseley took me about as far out of my comfort zone as I'm ever likely to go, but somehow I managed it without getting clipped and arrived at my brother's house by mid-afternoon.

Birmingham to Alcester via Llangollen

My brother and I are not alike – at least, that is what we both like to believe. He lives near the heart of Birmingham. As far as I can tell, he likes it there. I could no more live there than fly. Well, I suppose I could, but I know I wouldn't be happy.

I have never thought we looked alike, but as the years have passed the thinning and greying - or in my case, mostly loss - of our hair has helped to accentuate our similarities; enough at least to cause temporary confusion for his grand-children.

I parked the bike, took off my helmet and rang the door bell.

"Yes?" said my brother, looking puzzled at the clearly deranged person who had parked a motorcycle on his garden path.

"Can I help you?" ...."Oh, it's you. You're much bigger than I remember."

Only a couple of years had passed since I'd last visited, but in the world of families, little brothers are always, well, little. To find a vaguely familiar, but hulking motorcyclist blocking his front door must have seemed a bit strange. Nevertheless, identity confirmed, I was ushered inside for an evening of family catch-up, and a quick visit with Madeleine and John (whom we last met in Horton-in Ribblesdale) who just lived up the road.

It was a flying visit. I was eager to get back on the road. I had earmarked a couple of 'must do' rides and anyway, I couldn't wait to leave the urban sprawl behind.

I was heading for Wales, but first I had to extricate myself from the urban traffic. Shortly after leaving school I had briefly worked at the ailing BSA plant in Small Heath. We were living about half way between Stratford-on-Avon and Birmingham at the time, so my morning commute on my BSA C15 took me from the edge of the city, almost to its heart. At the time I didn't think about it much; it seemed perfectly normal to be dodging cars, braking hard for pedestrian crossings and diving around roundabouts - just as I had to now.

There's not much to distinguish where Birmingham ends and Bromsgrove begins, but beyond Bromsgrove, the narrow A448 was a bit more rural in nature. This was familiar territory; as a youth I had cycled and hitch-hiked this way many times, heading to Wales for a weekend of cycling or hiking.

I'm not sure much had changed. Although I didn't remember individual farms or views, somewhere in the recesses of my head I could feel familiarity. Like Kenneth Graham's Mole in *Wind of the Willows*, I caught a sense of something warm and very welcome which set my nerve endings tingling. It disappeared for a while through Kidderminster, I caught a whiff of it again as I passed substantial brick farmhouses and hedge lined fields along the floodplain of the River Teme, and it began to return strongly once I started to see timber framed cottages and hop fields.

Ludlow remains one of my favourite towns and holds a special place in my heart. When I was 12, my friend Christopher and I managed to talk our parents in to allowing us to ride the 50 miles to Ludlow, stay in the youth hostel overnight, then return the next day. It was my first big adventure; the first time I was out in the world and away from parental control. I now realise how hard it must have been for them to let their little baby, and it changed everything. After the Ludlow trip, I only ever went on holiday with my parents once; one taste of freedom and I was too busy exploring on my own.

In those days the roads were far less crowded and the wasn't the anxiety about child molesters behind every tree which immobilizes people these days. I'm sure my parents worried, but it was the biggest gift they could ever have given me.

Ludlow seemed little changed in 50 years. In the past I had almost always arrived after the long, fast and thrilling downhill from Clee Hill, so entering the town from the A49 was new and strange. The steep streets and ancient buildings were just the same; only the cars looked any different. I did a quick spin around the castle, stopped to take a picture of Broad Gate - the only remaining gate in the town wall - then headed out of town again.

The road north from Ludlow is busy and a bit ugly, but once I turned west at Craven Arms, things definitely improved. One of the great things about riding a motorcycle - especially one that has a sit-up-and-beg riding position - is that you sit up high above the road, you can see over the roofs of cars and over the hedgerows into the fields beyond. It was a green world of grass, winter wheat and ivy covered ancient field oaks, with low, dark hills rising on the horizon.

I stopped briefly in Clun to take advantage of the public facilities near the castle, narrowly beating a party of hikers, all of whom needed relief before heading for the trail. They had plenty trails to chose from: the Shropshire Way and the Jack Mytton Way both pass through Clun and Offas Dyke lies just a few miles west. Lovely, pastoral hiking, old forts on almost every hill top - they were in for a good day.

And so was I. The weather was cool but pleasant and the bike was perfectly suited to the narrow roads. I worked my way past Newtown then along minor roads to the village of Llanfair Caereinion where the smell of fish and chips emanating from Catrics Fish and Chip shop opposite the church stopped me in my tracks. I parked the bike just down the road and walked back. The smell was intoxicating.

Catrics Fish and Chip shop was indicative of some of the changes that have occurred throughout the UK as the whole country becomes more multi-cultural. The shop was a classic chippie, with formica and glass surfaces, ketchup and vinegar bottles and a row of canned pop on the shelf behind the till, but the people behind the counter were of Asian origin, not the white skinned, dark haired Welsh people I had been expecting.

I was served an enormous package of fish and chips, wrapped in the traditional grease proof paper and newspaper wrapping, which I ate on the wooden bench outside the town council office. It was wonderful.

I was heading for Lake Vernwy. This decidedly felt like Wales: there were sheep in almost every field, the grass was a rich green, the wooded hills were getting a little higher and the place names were unpronounceable. I filled up with fuel at the Dafarn Newydd Shop and Petrol Station before riding the last mile to the dam at the eastern end of the lake. Lake is a misnomer; reservoir is more accurate as there was no large water body in the Vernwy Valley until the world's first stone-built dam was completed across the valley in 1888 to provide water for Liverpool. It's not very often that one can describe industrial architecture as beautiful, but the Vernwy dam has a Gothic heaviness that fits the landscape perfectly. The Welsh Slate from which it is constructed blends organically with the surroundings and for some unknown reason, the turrets, ribs and arches don't jar.

It had started to rain; more of a fine mist really, which quickly covered and soaked everything. The dark grey, mossy rocks and the dam road were wet and grey cloud was hanging heavily over the water. The far end of the lake was invisible. All was quiet. I stowed my camera and saddled up again, heading along the southern shore road between Douglas Fir and Rhododendrons. The far side of the lake was all but invisible; only the vague shape of the hills looming through the mist showed that there was another shore. I was already wearing all the outer gear I possessed.

Three quarters of the way along the southern shore, a small road leads off towards the hills and the Bwlch y Groes pass, the second highest road in Wales, and another favourite of cyclists and motorcyclists. I had struggled up it from Dinas Mawddwy during a solo bicycle tour in my teenage, and was eager to see it again. In those days I loved to seek out and ride steep, isolated roads. I guess nothing much has changed.

I hadn't seen any vehicles since leaving the dam, so felt quite confident riding up the valley with one hand on the bars and the other recording a bit of video my camera. This may sound a bit daft, but I always loop the strap around my wrist and can instantly drop the camera if I have to make a grab for the bars.

The single track road winds up the edge of a valley onto open moorland with no hedges and no kerbs, finally emerging at the junction of the Bwlch y Groes pass. It was still raining, but the mist had lifted enough that I could see down the pass to the west, and see the road I would be taking to the north, snaking down the hillside. As I sat looking out over the moors and reading the sign board in the lay-by at the top of the pass the intensity of the rain noticeably increased. It was time to go.

Bala lay at the end of the valley; after that Llangollen. I won't bore you with the details of that long, wet ride through the gathering dark. By the time I had passed through Shrewsbury, Kidderminster (again) and Droitwich, I was looking for a pub, a motel, heck, even a hotel, but could find nothing. Eventually I stopped at the Roebuck Hotel in Alcester, only to be told that there were no rooms available and none for miles around; they were all booked solid because of the horse races in Cheltenham.

Perhaps I looked a bit desperate. Perhaps that North American twang worked in my favour, because the manager, who had been listening to my conversation with the receptionist said:

"Just hold on a minute sir, I might be able to sort something out".

While I drank a very welcome cup of coffee at the bar, he walked in to the back, returning a short while later with one of the staff and disappeared down the adjacent corridor. A couple of minutes later, they returned, the rather disgruntled looking girl dragging her bedding and belongings up to the upper floor.

"We've found you a room sir, if you'll just come this way".

The room was clean and tidy, relatively cheap and very, very welcome. Sometimes sounding like a foreigner can be useful!

Alcester to Norfolk

In the morning, I opened the curtain to see rain pouring down. The surfaces of all the puddles were alive with intersecting concentric rings as each rain drop added its weight to the water. The sky was heavy and grey; it looked as though it was in for the day.

I had a date with my friends in Norfolk, so there was nothing for it but to pull on my riding gear, strap my rucksack back on the bike and head east. Despite standing unprotected in the rain all night, the Royal

Enfield started straight away and was soon idling steadily as I tightened my chin strap and pulled on my mitts. They were still a bit soggy from the day before, but there wasn't much I could do about that, except to accept that I was going to have cold hands for the rest of the day. My boots were damp, but my new rain pants continued to be completely waterproof and my hiking gaiters diverted the water away from my feet.

I took the main road to Warwick, blasting along in the spray from early morning commuter traffic, then turned towards the town centre. Not surprisingly, there was a line of traffic spreading back from a main intersection so I dutifully kept my position in line, only to be passed by two cyclists and another motorcycle who rode up the centre-line. I had forgotten all about filtering; it's an alien concept in Canada, where even if you are on two wheels, you're expected to wait your turn like everyone else.

After I was passed by a second bike, I decided I would give it a try myself and pulled out into the centre of the road. Not only did nobody beep their horn at me; one or two cars even moved over slightly to ensure that I had enough room to navigate. Within seconds I was at the head of the line, and as soon as the lights changed, I was away. I was liking this, and kicked myself for not trying it before.

Leamington passed in a blur of traffic and puddles and before long I was heading towards Daventry. This was old familiar territory again. Years ago, when I lived in Norfolk, I rode these roads to see my mother every other weekend. Had it not been for the rain, I would have been having fun. Oh heck, I was having fun anyway.

After a wet slog along the busy dual carriageway past Northampton, I stopped near Higham Ferrers to wring out my gloves. The rain had finally stopped, the sky was brightening and while is wasn't what you might call warm, the weather certainly looked more promising.

It's really just a short ride from Warwickshire to Norfolk and despite the wet start I was well ahead of schedule. My friends were working all day and would not be home until supper time, so there was no point in me arriving too early. Instead of heading straight to their house, I did what any sensible person would do and headed for the pub. Not just any old pub, of course: I made for the Ostrich in Castle Acre once again.

I sat nursing a pint of Greene King Ostrich Ale - well, I had to have that, didn't I? - and demolished a few packets of crisps. It was not my intention to eavesdrop on other people's conversations, but I could hardly avoid over-hearing that the young guy behind the bar was soon to be married. As is so often the case, he was being counselled to avoid it by a couple of guys who, from the stories they recounted, had clearly not enjoyed their relationships. Eventually they left. As I headed for the door I caught the eye of the bartender and said:

"In a few days, I'll have been married 35 years and we're still happy. Don't let the doom and gloom boys give you cold feet".

I killed a little more time looking around Castle Acre then headed back to Swaffam to fill the remaining holes in my pack and panniers with beer and wine before moving on to arrive at my friends.

The day and two nights I spent with them doesn't really form part of this tale. Suffice it say that a goodly amount of beer was consumed, a number of fine medieval churches were visited and I had the best venison haunch supper a man could eat.

Norfolk to Yorkshire

My time in the UK was rapidly coming to a close. I was scheduled to return the bike to D & C by 9AM on Monday morning which left me with Sunday as a travelling. day to ride the 200 miles back up to Yorkshire. During the years I have been away, many of the A roads have become over-trafficed and a bit bleak - at least for a rider like me. Nevertheless, with the promise of limited Sunday traffic, I stuck to the A17 past King's Lynn and headed north. There weren't too many 'Sunday Drivers' out and about; the weather was chilly, damp and grey and far too uninspiring to seduce them from the couch.

I'd been able to completely dry my boots and gloves on my friends kitchen Rayburn, so it took longer than usual for the cold to penetrate, but by the time I reached Sleaford I was more than ready for a few minutes in the warm, nursing a mug of hot chocolate. Once again I cursed McDonalds for their absurd WiFi policy - but I enjoyed the hot chocolate, so I shouldn't bad-mouth them too much.

At Marton, a few miles further on, I stopped again. The unusual church tower had caught my eye as I rode through the village. It's not often that you see a church tower completely built of alternating rows of small slabs in a herringbone pattern and it looked old to me. My intuition was right; the sign board outside the church described the tower as 11th century, with a mix of Anglo-Saxon and Norman elements. I didn't remember it at the time, but my father's side of the family are from a small group of villages in the vicinity of Marton and lived in the area for so many centuries that I like to think they grew autochthonously from the primordial Lincolnshire mud. I wonder whether I was feeling some deeply sub-conscious resonance, and it was that which encouraged me to stop and not the church tower at all.

I don't know why, but I was expecting more from Gainsborough. Perhaps I was thinking of the famous 18th century portrait and landscape painter Thomas Gainsborough and assumed that a place with the same name would have grown up around a whole crop of ancient and architecturally interesting buildings. Instead, all I saw was rank upon rank of yellow and red brick houses; some older, some newer, but none charming. Perhaps the dull day was getting to me.

Somewhere along the road between Crowle and Goole, I stopped at a pub for some lunch, only to be informed that other than a bag of crisps, there wasn't anything available - some story about a catered lunch, invitation only - so I downed a quick pint of cider and resumed my journey.

Goole (I still love that name), Selby, Tadcaster and Wetherby all went by without making any kind of impression on me. People often express wonder that I can ride for hour after hour through the stunted trees of the relatively featureless boreal forest in Canada without getting bored, yet I was finding the unchanging landscape of fields, hedgerows, stone walls and grassy verges, interspersed every few yards with brick and slate house and farms, a bit wearing. Three weeks of being constantly on the move must have finally got to me. I needed to be somewhere where I could put my feet up - somewhere that felt like home. The trouble was, I was no longer sure that such a place existed. Everything about Britain felt familiar yet it wasn't quite home any longer, any more than Canada completely felt like home despite the many years I'd lived there. I'd become a mid-Atlantic person, with no earth beneath my feet I could call my own.

Just as I started to sink into a grim mood I noticed a middle aged, balding guy moving to stand at the very edge of the road. At first I thought he was going to cross, but as I got closer, I could see his broad grin as he started to clap and give me the thumbs up. No facetiousness here; he was genuinely happy to see me rolling by. I don't know whether he thought the Royal Enfield was vintage, whether he was applauding me for touring in the cold of March, or some combination thereof. It didn't matter. Whatever it was, it made him happy – and that made me happy too.

The rest of the day passed in a blur of A roads, traffic and suburban houses. I weathered Harrogate then headed west along the Skipton Road. The first part of the road is remarkably straight - not surprising, given it's Roman origins - and runs past school football fields and endless housing estates. Eventually the road broke out into open country of flat green fields, dry stone walls and Hawthorne trees with the occasional stone or brick farm thrown in for good measure. Towards Blubberhouses the land started to develop a bit of a roll and in the absence of urban sprawl, I was content to be rolling along, the bike pumping away beneath me uncomplainingly, although after a long day in the saddle, I had become thoroughly chilled and my backside was eager for a rest.

I'd been keeping my eye out for somewhere to stay, but the few places I passed looked too 'tony' for my tastes so I suffered a bit longer and carried on to Skipton.

I immediately liked Skipton. I'm a bit of a sucker for a broad High Street lined with cobbled parking areas, uniform stone shops and pubs and a modest and comfortable look, not overly focussed on serving the needs of tourists and visitors from away.

Just down the Keithley Road and over the canal, I found a terrace of brown stone houses, about every second one of which seemed to be a B&B. I parked at the first gap in parked cars, opened the gate of the closest B&B and rang the bell. I always seem to get the same stunned look - perhaps it's my bedraggled appearance, although it's probably just that no one is expecting walk-in trade in early March - but after a mere moment's hesitation, I was welcomed inside, shown to a warm and comfortable top floor room and given an exhaustive run down on all the international visitors who had stayed there over the last few years. I was going to be warm and dry for my last night on the road, even if my ears ached.

I was a bit concerned about leaving the bike unattended on the side of the road, despite the landlady's assurances that it would be fine. Anyway, with D & C's boat chain and factory gate padlock around the front wheel, any casual thief was going to have a heck of a time wheeling it away.

After a shower, a cup of coffee and a bit of evening TV, I hobbled back down-town to see what I could find to eat. My tolerance for pub food had reached it's limit; I was far more interested in the entrancing smells coming from a Pakistani take-out across the canal. I had to wait for a while, but the chicken Balti I eventually received was worth it. I think I must have accidentally ordered the family meal, because there was an endless vat of meat and sauce and two large nan. It was a struggle, but I managed to get it all down while sitting on the low wall watching the traffic roll by.

In he morning I rode with the morning traffic down the Keithley Road, filled the bike's fuel tank then rode the last few miles to Cowling. The Royal Enfield was no longer as sparklingly clean as it had been when I picked it us, but Dave didn't seem to mind. He gave a quick check over as I removed my rucksack and emptied the panniers then gave me a lift to the train station in Colne so that I could catch the train to Manchester. Eventually I made my way to Manchester Airport, killed some more time in the departures lounge then took off across the Atlantic. As the plane reached cruising altitude and the passengers began to settle down once the excitement of the in-flight meal was over, I wondered when, or even if I would see the UK again.

Another Royal Enfield - same weather. In Settle, buying rain pants.

Actually, I'm English

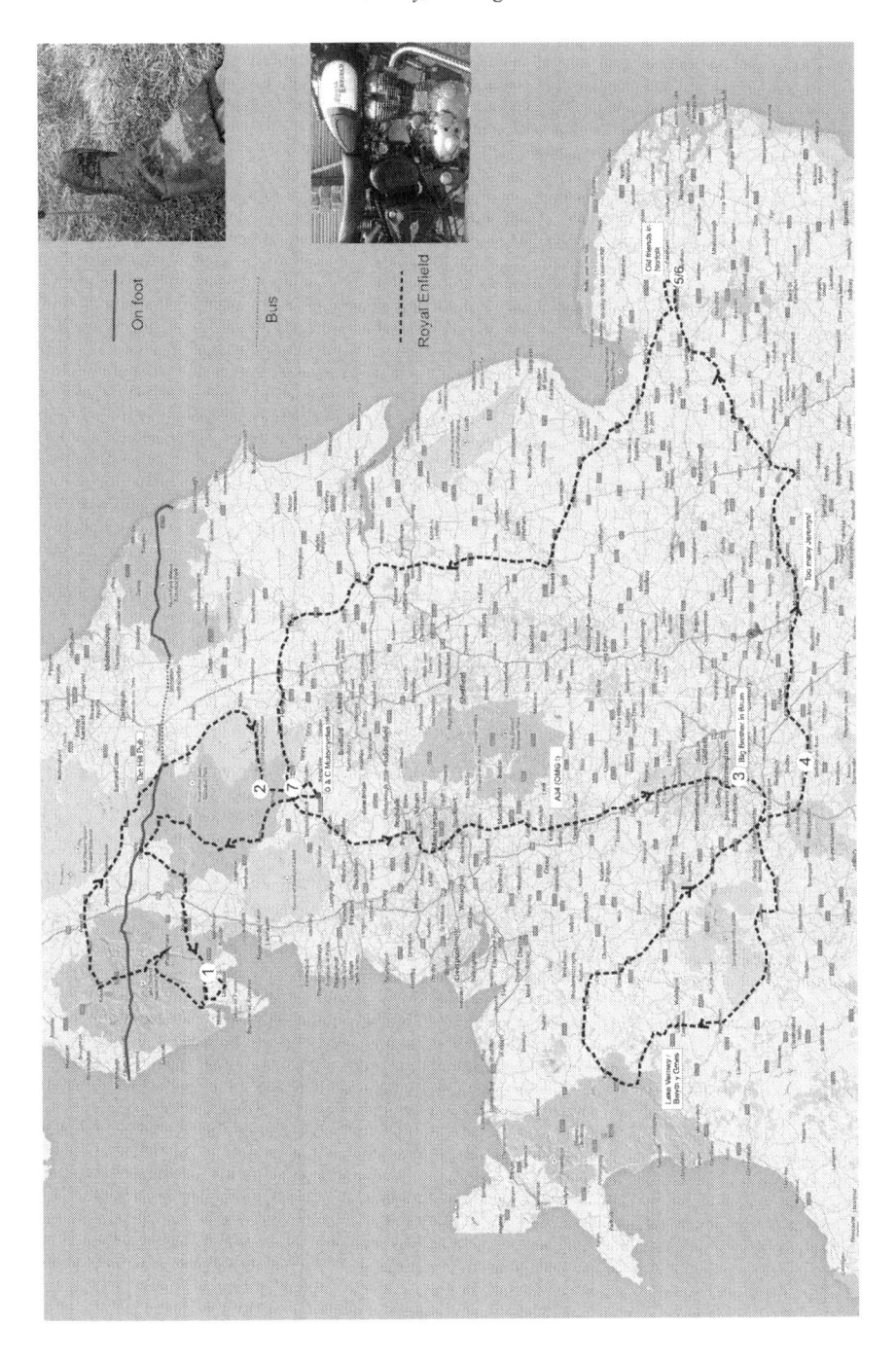

Heading into Wales

POSTSCRIPT

According to recent statistics, Britain has become one of the most densely populated countries in Europe, with 60 million people crowded in to 93,278 square miles. Extract the large and sparsely populated uplands of Scotland from those figures and the numbers really jump, to an average of over 1000 people per square mile. With numbers like that, you would think you would be tripping over people to find a few square inches of breathing space, yet throughout my hiking trips I was able to find quiet and isolation, often walking all day without seeing another soul. I realise that February and March are not considered optimal hiking season by most, but if you are looking to get away from the urban crush, they are fine months to do it. If I'd been hiking during the summer, things would almost certainly have been different.

However, isolation and remoteness are an illusion. The reality is, you're never really very far from anywhere. Most of the time, whether walking through Wales, along the spine of the Pennines or from one side of the country to the other, there are always villages, farms, even towns and cities within a few miles. I had to suppress a chuckle when I read that the Black Sail Youth Hostel in Ennerdale, was one of the most isolated hostels in the UK; it's nearest neighbour is 4 miles down the valley and the nearest village a whole 6 miles away. Of course, when the weather closes in, the winds begin to howl and the temperature drops, you might just as well be in the Arctic – except the Arctic doesn't have a cosy pub just down the road.

During the various trips I describe in these chapters, I deliberately avoided as many cities, towns and major roads as I could. It's not always possible though. Inevitably you find yourself in the urban mix sooner or later, whether you like it or not. And I don't like it. Compared to what I remember, the cities seem bigger, a little grimier and decidedly more busy. I didn't like them before I moved to Canada; I don't like them now.

When you abandon your former homeland, no matter how much you like your new country, there is always a nagging feeling in the back of your mind that perhaps you should have stayed at home. Would I have been happier, more affluent, smarter, more adventurous had I stayed in the UK? I don't know. I'm content with my life in Canada – but it's certainly nice to get home once in a while.

ABOUT THE AUTHOR

Nick Adams emigrated to Canada from the UK in 1977 to work for the Ontario government as an archaeologist. He soon fell in love with Canada's north and, for the past few years, has been exploring it by canoe and on his beloved 1970's Moto Guzzi motorcycles.

From time to time, he returns to the UK to 'get a breath of Britain' by hiking some of its many long-distance footpaths and riding around visiting friends and relatives on Royal Enfield motorcycles.

Writing about his trips and sharing them with others doubles the pleasure. He is a regular contributor to 'RealClassic' magazine and frequently posts to on-line motorcycle forums.

A welcome sign

If you enjoyed reading this, you might also enjoy my other book, available in Kindle and Paperback formats:

Beyond the Coffee Shop: Riding 1970's Moto Guzzis in Northern Canada

"Canada is blessed with thousands of kilometres of empty roads which seem to wind on forever through forested hills and between still blue lakes. What better way to explore them than by riding 40 year old Italian motorbikes, famous for their dodgy electrics and sparse dealer network. 40 year old bikes, aged rider, thousands of kilometres of virtually unserviced empty roads in the middle of bear, wolf and blackfly infested wilderness - what could possibly go wrong?"

Printed in Great Britain
by Amazon.co.uk, Ltd.,
Marston Gate.